THE HIRING HANDBOOK
FOR PET SITTERS AND DOG WALKERS

How to Find, Hire, and Keep the Best Staff for Your Pet Sitting and Dog Walking Business

KRISTIN MORRISON

OTHER BOOKS BY KRISTIN MORRISON:

Six-Figure Pet Sitting:
Catapult Your Pet Sitting Business
to Unlimited Success

Six-Figure Pet Business:
Unleash the Potential in Your Dog Training,
Pet Grooming and Doggy Day Care Business

Prosperous Pet Business:
Interviews with the Experts: Volume One

30 Days to Start and Grow
Your Pet Sitting and Dog Walking Business:
A Step-By-Step Guide to Launch, Attract Clients,
and Make a Profit

THE HIRING HANDBOOK FOR PET SITTERS AND DOG WALKERS

"*Kristin Morrison has written a powerful 'next step' book for pet sitters and dog walkers!* The Hiring Handbook for Pet Sitters and Dog Walkers *is an A-to-Z guide for finding the right employees and what to do once you've found the right ones, as well as how to handle the wrong ones. Kristin delves into the world of independent contractors and gives sage advice on dealing with them as well. If you're looking to add staff, this is a must-read from a seasoned professional in the pet industry.*"

Yvette Gonzales
Past President, National Association
of Professional Pet Sitters (NAPPS)

"*Next to starting a business, expansion and hiring can be the most daunting hurdles for owners to cross. Thankfully,* The Hiring Handbook for Pet Sitters and Dog Walkers *turns the seemingly daunting and overwhelming task of hiring and training into an easy, approachable endeavor.* The Hiring Handbook for Pet Sitters and Dog Walkers *is a timely, necessary read to help pet care providers identify what their business needs, learn how to screen and interview candidates, and retain talented personnel. Whether you're hiring your first employee or expanding to a new location, Kristin Morrison's advice is positive, practical, encouraging, and actionable.*"

Pet Sitters Associates, LLC
Business Insurance for Pet Sitters

"Whether you are a seasoned pet business owner with many staff members or just getting ready to hire your first, you'll find Kristin Morrison's latest book, The Hiring Handbook for Pet Sitters and Dog Walkers, *invaluable! Hiring can be a daunting prospect for any business owner, but in the pet care industry especially, we want to guard our hard-earned reputation while finding excellent, trustworthy people who want to help us succeed. Kristin has firsthand experience in running her own prosperous pet sitting and dog walking business, and this book is a collection of her learnings and practical knowledge from actually being 'in the trenches'. Kristin's book arms pet business owners with strategies that work while avoiding the pitfalls and costly mistakes.* The Hiring Handbook for Pet Sitters and Dog Walkers *contains a wealth of vital information for your hiring success, yet it is an easy and pleasant read. I highly recommend it."*

Jan McDonnal
Tracy, California

"Once again Kristin has written a most engaging and informative book. Her knowledge, passion, and caring shine through on every page packed with inspiration and invaluable information for success. This book is like having your very own mentor to guide you and supporter to help you and your business reach your full potential. Thank you, Kristin."

Kirsty Everard
Kirsty's Paws
Bournemouth, Dorset, England

"I absolutely loved this book! I had no idea how to hire employees, or when. Just the thought scared me to death! Kristin makes this book so easy and enjoyable to read, and it tells you everything you need to know!"

Jan Sutton
Snoring Moose Pet Services
Greeley, Colorado

"The Hiring Handbook for Pet Sitters and Dog Walkers *came at a perfect time for me and my business. I was feeling overworked and overwhelmed with the prospect of hiring. This book gave me the pep talk I needed and the action steps and confidence I needed to hire in the right way for my business. From posting the job ad all the way through to introducing new hires to my clients,* The Hiring Handbook *was such a huge help! Thank you!"*

Polly Goode
Polly's Adventure Walks
Portland, Oregon

"This is the best book out there for anyone wanting to know the specific steps needed for hiring and keeping the best staff. Not only are there hiring tips within each chapter, but there are also Action Steps at the end of each chapter, as well as a Question and Answer section at the end of the book. You'll find out exactly how to hire the very best staff, who is the best fit for your business, and how to keep those great staff members!"

Dee Kate Murdock
Leash and Collar Dog Services
Lubbock, Texas

"The Hiring Handbook for Pet Sitters and Dog Walkers *is the perfect guide to walk you step-by-step through the entire hiring process, start to finish! Kristin makes it so simple and takes the guesswork out of everything for you. You'll wonder why you haven't already hired yet."*

Angela Wilkinson
Jet Set Pet Sitters, LLC
Portland, Oregon

"Kristin's books never disappoint, and this one is no exception! This book brings together all the facets of hiring good staff for pet businesses. It is a manual that shows step by step when, why, and how to hire and keep staff members for the long term. With her background in having hired many staff members in her own pet sitting and dog walking business, her guidance is truly priceless. A must-read for all pet business owners growing beyond what they can do themselves."

Kelly Catlett
Waggs 2 Whiskers, LLC
Bagdad, Kentucky

"This book is a wealth of detailed and useful information for any owner of a pet sitting or dog walking business; the information has been clearly gleaned from years of experience both as a business owner and as a coach of pet business owners. Especially helpful are the extremely detailed "Action Steps". Some are brainstorming thought exercises; others are concrete steps such as forms that need to be filled out and calls to action that need to be made. In some places, there is even actual wording to use in communicating your hiring decisions to clients and employees. Kristin Morrison has thought through many different hiring scenarios and has advice for each of them."

Stacy Brawlau-Schneck
Stacy's Wag'N'Train
San Jose, California

"Should I hire someone to help me instead of doing all the work myself? THAT is the question, and THIS book will answer it! Every chapter is chock-full of valuable information. Having read The Hiring Handbook for Pet Sitters and Dog Walkers, I now know I'm ready to make the leap! Thanks, Kristin."

Christine Stutz
The Cat's Pajamas Cat Sitting
Minneapolis, Minnesota

"Wow! After reading Kristin Morrison's Hiring Handbook for Pet Sitters and Dog Walkers, I can't wait to implement her strategies! The Action Steps at the end of each chapter will make it so easy to efficiently navigate the process of hiring staff, and I am very much looking forward to taking these steps. I'm definitely guilty of letting fear stop me from moving forward with my business in this regard, despite lucking out several years ago and finding one perfect staff member–I'm afraid I'll never find anyone as perfect as she is! I know I need more help, and I am now motivated and energized to getting on with it. Thanks, Kristin, for putting out such a helpful manual for pet business owners once again!"

Lawana Quest
Cat's Cradle Critter Sitter
Surrey, BC, Canada

No part of this book may be reproduced in any form or by any electronic or mechanical means, including information storage and retrieval systems, or be sold or resold, without permission in writing from the author. The only exception is that a reviewer may quote short excerpts in a review.

Limit of Liability / Disclaimer of Warranty: While the publisher and author have used their best efforts in preparing this book, they make no representations or warranties, express or implied, with respect to the accuracy or completeness of the contents of this book or otherwise, and specifically disclaim any implied warranties, including any implied warranties of merchantability or fitness for a particular purpose. There are no warranties which extend beyond the descriptions contained in this paragraph. No warranties may be created or extended by sales representatives or written sales materials. The information provided herein and the opinions stated herein are not guaranteed or warranted to produce any particular results, and the advice and strategies contained herein are not suitable for every individual and may not be suitable for your situation. You should consult with a professional where appropriate. By providing information or links to other companies or websites, the publisher and the author do not guarantee, approve, or endorse the information or products available at any linked websites or mentioned companies or persons. This publication is designed to provide information with regard to the subject matter covered. It is sold or provided with the understanding that neither the publisher nor the author is engaged in rendering legal, accounting, or other professional services. If legal advice or other expert assistance is required, the services of a competent professional should be sought. Neither the publisher nor the author shall be liable for any loss or loss of profit or any other commercial damages, including but not limited to special, incidental, consequential, or other damages.

The Hiring Handbook for Pet Sitters and Dog Walkers

To my precious mother-in-law, Marilouise Jackson.

Kind and generous heart,

Maternal wings that comfort those in need,

Pathfinder,

Empathic leader,

Curious mind and spirit,

Loving mom to the man I'm blessed to share my life with,

Thank you for this — and for so much more.

Table of Contents

Appreciation

As I think about all who have helped me deliver this book into being, I'm sitting in front of my office fireplace with a big wood fire that's putting off a lot of cozy heat on this cold winter day. I've written some of this book while in Big Sur on my once-a-month writing retreat, but my home office is where I have written most of this book. The power of place is important to me (I think it is to a lot of writers — and perhaps to most people), so I want to start off my gratitude by acknowledging this warm and inviting place in my home that has helped fuel a lot of my creativity!

This book would certainly not have been possible without Kimberly M. — editor and exquisite wordsmith. She had some hardships in the midst of the writing of this book and, in spite of those hardships, she was still such a believer in the value of this book that she pressed on in spite of all she was going through. Her direction and gentle guidance have been the rudders that brought this book to fruition. Thank you so much, dear Kimberly.

Thank you to the pet sitters and dog walkers who happily volunteered to be early readers of the book and generously gave their suggestions: Jan M., Jan S., Christine S., Angela W., Kelly C., Stacey B., Lawana Q., Polly G., Dee M., Kirsty E., and Elizabeth D. Your feedback was invaluable. Thank you so much!

A big dose of gratitude to the 250+ people I hired during the course of running my 18-year pet business. Thanks to all I learned through the process of finding, hiring, and training all of you — this book is here because of you.

I've been a part of a powerful community of business owners for over 15 years now, and I'm deeply grateful for my Thursday Business Support Group. Though the writing of all my books has happened in solitude, my powerful business-owner tribe has been cheering me on from the sidelines during the writing of every single book, from start to finish, including this one — my fifth book!

I feel lucky to have such supportive and loving friends: Adva M., Marie Y., Sheira K., Susan G., Cynthia S., Sharon E., Sunya A., Terra C., Alicia D., and Lorraine P.

My team of virtual assistants keeps me facing in the right direction with all my various projects, and I'm immensely grateful: Tonie L. is a fantastic webmistress—I've been lucky to have her on my team for many, many years and she's such a gift. Diana S. and Sharon S. help me do so many things, including getting my weekly newsletter out to my email subscribers, creating the Prosperous Pet Business Online Conference, and so many other tasks that they put their hearts and souls into. Paul T. is my Prosperous Pet Business podcast editor and makes it possible for pet business owners from all over the world to listen and learn from my podcast when they are driving, walking dogs, or doing the dishes. If you've listened to the podcast, you, dear reader, have Paul to thank for delivering it to you!

And last but definitely not least, my beloved husband Spencer. In addition to his stable, solid love and support, he lightens me up and makes me laugh many times every day. Having a successful business is a wonderful thing and, to me, having a simpatico partner to walk through life with is even better.

Before You Begin...

In the pages that follow, you will find all the information I wish I'd had when I was first hiring and training dog walkers and pet sitters in my own pet business, as well as valuable lessons I learned in the process of taking my business from a one-person business to a company that had 35 staff members and could thrive without me while I traveled for months at a time each year.

But before we begin, I'd like to share my story so you will know who I am and why you can trust me to guide you on your hiring journey.

I started a pet sitting and dog walking business in 1995 and grew it to be one of the largest pet care companies in Northern California. In 2000, I began coaching pet sitters and dog walkers in addition to running my business. I sold my business in 2013 to focus even more of my time on helping pet sitters and dog walkers achieve success. Since then, I have continued coaching pet care business owners through my books, seminars, webinars, online programs, the annual Prosperous Pet Business Online Conference, and the Prosperous Pet Business podcast.

When I first started my pet sitting and dog walking company, I had no prior experience running a business. Although the job seemed like a good fit for my skills and love of animals, I made many mistakes along the way.

A few years into running my business, I was overwhelmed and burned out. I felt like I was giving more and more each week to my business without any relief. I had no life outside of my business and I was ready to quit. And in spite of what felt like working all the time, I was somehow not making much money. Does any of that sound familiar to you? If so, don't worry. There is a better way to run a pet sitting and dog walking business and still have a personal life!

Instead of throwing in the towel, I gave myself one year to fix my business. I still loved the work I was doing, but I knew I needed to change a number of things if I was going to continue to serve my clients *and* have a personal life that I enjoyed. I dedicated the next 365 days to my top three goals: change the way I ran my business, increase my quality of life, and make a lot more money.

I spent that year exploring different ways to run my business and create more personal time so I had a life again. I studied everything from the nuts and bolts of business administration to the psychology of what my clients really wanted and how to offer our services without being pushy. What a turning point that year was! By the end of the year, I was enjoying my life again and I had made more money in that one year of focused intention than I had in the previous two years combined.

One of the most incredible outcomes of my year of change was how much easier it was to run my business. For the first time since starting my business, I had time to myself again. Before selling my company, I was working just two or three days a week and traveling for multiple months each year. I was able to explore parts of the world that I'd always wanted to visit without my business suffering in my absence. Instead, my business thrived! I had shaped my company to run without me there to oversee every detail. So much of this newfound freedom came from hiring and training the very best staff members.

I've seen business owners make many of the same hiring mistakes that I had made early in my business. I find them experiencing some of the same challenges I had in the early days of my own business, including mistakes and misconceptions about hiring and staffing when it comes time to expand. My goal with this book is to help you avoid the hiring mistakes I made and the staffing problems many of my coaching clients come to me to fix. The information in this book will give you the tools you need to find, hire, and keep the very best employees to achieve long-term success in your pet sitting and/or dog walking business. I will teach you the necessary steps to build your business by hiring in a way that enables you the time to enjoy your family and friends, travel, be creative, and have a personal life outside of your business.

Each chapter that follows will give you practical suggestions for confidently hiring and managing employees. I will also share *Hiring Success Stories* from pet sitting and dog walking business owners that relate to each chapter's topic. These are people who have been where you are now, and many of them have experienced the life-changing results from the same tips you will find in this book. At the end of each chapter, I've also included glimpses into my own business journey so you can learn from the experience I gained while running my own business.

As you read, pay attention to the *Hiring Tips*. Each chapter contains a particularly empowering suggestion that will help you throughout the hiring, training, and managing process. If you end up owning your business for a number of years, you will find yourself hiring and training many employees throughout the life of your business. These *Hiring Tips* will be regular sources of support—you will be able to flip back through the book each time you prepare to hire or when you encounter a new staffing challenge in the future.

You do not need to finish this book before you start applying what you are learning to your own pet sitting and dog walking business. At the end of each chapter, I've listed *Action Steps* for you to complete. These are practical, measurable steps for you to take while you are reading this book to find the staff members you need as soon as possible. And if you are already at a different stage of your hiring journey than the very beginning, feel free to jump ahead to the chapter that offers the specific guidance you need.

At the end of this book, you will find a *Q&A* section that answers actual questions I've been asked while coaching pet business owners through the hiring process. If you have a specific question in mind already, you will probably find a succinct answer there.

Now that you know what to expect from this book, it's time to get started! Here are the very first *Action Steps*, a few crucial steps to take before you begin with Chapter One:

Action Step

Join the private Facebook group for readers of *The Hiring Handbook for Pet Sitters and Dog Walkers* at:
www.facebook.com/groups/PetSitHiringHandbook.

Action Step

Designate a special journal or notebook for taking notes and completing the *Action Steps* and other exercises in this book. This "hiring success journal" will be a great resource for you while you work through this book and beyond. You will find that having all of your thoughts and records of your progress in one place will help you stay organized and motivated. Keeping track of what you do and the progress you make each day will help you feel a sense of accomplishment and keep you motivated. Writing down your ideas, *Action Steps*, and goals is so much more powerful than simply thinking about them.

Action Step

Some of the *Action Steps* in this book will require that you use a timer. It is also very helpful to have a timer handy to keep you on track while you work each day. Purchase a dedicated timer for use throughout this book. I recommend using a timer other than your smartphone timer, so you do not get distracted by texts, phone calls, or social media. Instead, purchase a timer that is specifically used for this hiring process. Get creative! This is a good way to bring a personal and lighthearted touch to your workspace. You will find pictures of fun and unusual timers in the private Facebook group to get some great ideas. Post a picture of your new timer there, too!

Action Step

Find someplace comfortable where you can write without interruption and set your dedicated timer for 10 minutes. Whatever you do, keep writing continually until your timer rings. This is the first of many times I will ask you to use your hiring success journal to explore how you feel about a particular aspect of your pet sitting and dog walking business. During these exploration sessions, don't worry about grammar, proper punctuation, or writing in complete sentences. If you run out of words to write, keep your pen moving anyway. Take a cue from professional writers who know that the act of simply writing the same word over and over again will keep their brains focused on the task at hand and can encourage a burst of inspiration. You may be surprised to find that you think of more things than you expected after your initial burst of writing.

When you are ready to begin, make two lists:

- First, make a list of anything that is making you uncomfortable or unhappy in your business right now. If you are the only person working in your business currently, include the ways that you feel overwhelmed or stretched too thin. If you already have staff, be sure to include anything you do not like about the way they fit within your business or any frustrations you have dealing with their scheduling or management.

- Second, make a list of the ways you would spend your energy if you had more available time in each week, month, or year. What do you feel excited to do in your personal life that you just don't have time for right now? And if you simply need to relax, nap, and eat bonbons because you've been working so hard growing your business, that's fine, too! Put it down on the list.

This is your chance to articulate what is working currently, as well as to visualize what you will be able to do and change once you've successfully hired and trained stellar employees. You will find it helpful to have these specific ideas and goals to refer back to throughout the process.

ONE

Why You Need to Hire (and When)

The Benefits of Hiring and How to Know It's Time

"If you hire good people, give them good jobs, and pay them good wages, generally something good is going to happen."

–James Sinegal

At some point, every small business owner is faced with an exciting and slightly terrifying question: "Should I hire someone to help me instead of doing all the work myself?" There is something exciting about the idea that this business you've created and nurtured is busy enough to justify expanding. On the other hand, the idea of giving up even a little bit of control can make many business owners hesitant to hire. In this chapter, I will go over the many benefits of hiring help to inspire you to move forward. I will also teach you how to identify whether you and your business are ready to take that step.

The Benefits of Hiring Help

Hiring the right people to help you with your business has many advantages, most of which come down to one of three main benefits. Hiring good staff will (1) let you be the visionary at the helm of your business "ship" rather than always working in the belly of the ship; (2) give you more time for your personal life, including time for family, friends, self-care, and hobbies; and (3) increase your profits by allowing your business to serve more clients (and serve them better).

Focus on the Big Picture

It is so easy to get bogged down in the day-to-day needs of your business that you never take a step back and plan for your business's future. Once you have hired and trained the right employees, you will be able to hand over some of the regular responsibilities and gain the necessary time to focus on the big picture. When you are not inundated with the responsibilities of managing your business on top of completing all of the day-to-day pet care yourself, you will have the time and mental space to gain much-needed perspective. You will be able to make decisions about the direction of your business and intentionally choose where to focus your energy and resources. You may be surprised at how many aspects of your business you can nurture once you are not the only person running the show.

Once you have hired exceptional staff members, you will be free to do the following:

- Take a step back and evaluate what is working in your business and what still needs improvement.

- Sign up for a workshop or webinar to help you build business skills.

- Establish long-term goals for profit, marketing, and business expansion.

- Spend time building community and networking relationships that will lead to better name and brand recognition for your business, as well as cultivate satisfying connections in your business community.

Enjoy More Time

Once you hire and train the right staff, you will have more time for your business and for your personal life. I first decided to hire help for my own business when I realized I couldn't do it all myself. Not only that, but I also realized that I *didn't want to do it all*. When I started building my business to run without me overseeing every minute of every day, I discovered something important. While I had started the business because I love animals, caring for them seven days a week was exhausting.

Look back at the list you made in your hiring success journal of the things you would do if you had more time in each week, month, or year. How much more fulfilling would your life be if your business could function without you one, two, or three days each week? What if you could leave the country for an entire summer while still making a profit and come home to a thriving business and happy, satisfied clients? With the right hiring practices in place and staff to help you, you will be amazed at how much more time you will have to enjoy your life. In the *Action Steps* at the end of this chapter, you will have the opportunity to add even more to the list you made earlier.

Serve More Clients, Better

Have you ever had to turn down a potential pet sitting client because you were already booked for the week in question? Are you booked with clients during the prime hours for dog walks (generally 11 am-2 pm)? Would you like to take on more dog walking clients, but you can't? Do you have periods during busy seasons (summers and holidays, for example) where you have large numbers of clients call last minute, desperate to find a pet sitter? Are you booked to capacity and turning down requests for new appointments? If you answered any of these questions with a *yes*, your business is probably ready for more help.

The surprising truth is that you may be ready to hire employees even if you don't already have more work than you can manage. When you have more available hours and days for pet sitting and dog walking jobs, thanks to a few additional employees, you will be able to actively market your business to fill up those slots. I have consistently found that my coaching clients who are willing to hire just slightly more help than they think they need are often able to quickly find more clients than they imagined possible. When you provide a larger time, space, or staff "container" for your business, it's likely to get filled. Remember: nature abhors a vacuum!

Not only will hiring employees enable you to fit more clients on your business schedule, but you will also be able to dedicate more time and energy to give your existing clients what they really want. When all of the day-to-day operations fall on your shoulders alone, it can be difficult to find the time to handle customer complaints or suggestions, put out "fires", or evaluate client feedback and take action when needed. Your relationship with your clients will thrive when you have at least a couple of extra hours each day to answer emails, return phone calls, and address problems as they arise ... and without the panic that sets in when a customer calls right as you are walking out the door to get to another dog walking or pet sitting appointment.

> NOT ONLY WILL HIRING EMPLOYEES ENABLE YOU TO FIT MORE CLIENTS ON YOUR BUSINESS SCHEDULE, BUT YOU WILL ALSO BE ABLE TO DEDICATE MORE TIME AND ENERGY TO GIVE YOUR EXISTING CLIENTS WHAT THEY REALLY WANT.

Nine Signs It's Time to Hire

If you still aren't sure if it's the right time for your business to add staff members, consider the following signs that it's time to hire:

1. You are losing your passion (and your patience) for your business. When I started my pet sitting and dog walking business, I was excited about doing the work I loved and being my own boss. A few years in, however, I found I had lost my enthusiasm. Even though I still loved my pet clients (and their humans) and enjoyed the freedom of being self-employed, I was no longer excited about my business. This is not unusual for small business owners, especially in service industries like pet care. If you feel like you've lost the passion that drove you to start your business in the first place, you may be trying to do too much on your own.

2. You feel like you can't take a day off without your business suffering. Vacations and sick days are impossible for pet sitters and dog walkers who do all the work themselves. Hiring the right employees will give you more time for yourself: the ability to stay home and take care of yourself when you are ill, freedom to take a vacation without losing income, and time to simply take a day off to rest.

3. You are turning down new clients. One surefire sign that your business is ready for additional employees is that you find yourself regularly turning down new clients. If you find yourself saying "no" to new business or end up booking more visits or walks than you can personally handle during busy times of the year, it's time to be realistic about what you can actually handle by yourself. You will need to hire help if you want to avoid reducing the number of clients you take.

4. You spend more time putting out fires than working on what's truly important. It can be very easy to spend so much time juggling the demands of office work with the actual pet visits and dog walks (not to mention dealing with urgent issues that arise daily) that you don't give yourself enough time for other professional or personal ventures. Urgent work, such as returning client calls and emails in a timely manner, often crowds out the most important tasks that don't have pending deadlines. Hiring employees to share the workload will give you the time you need for less urgent (but important) tasks.

5. Some of your customers are unhappy. Have you been getting more client complaints than usual? If you are overworked and stretched too thin, the quality of your work may be suffering. Even if the complaints are unjustified, you may not be giving as much time to customer service as your clients need if you are trying to do everything yourself.

6. You feel annoyed, discouraged, or overwhelmed by all the work you have to do. Do you feel a jolt of anxiety or frustration when the business phone rings or an email comes in? When you start your work each day, are you excited or annoyed? Evaluating how you feel throughout the workweek will give you a clear picture of whether or not your business needs more staff members to share the workload.

7. Your business needs specialized skills you don't have. Your hiring need not be limited to simply bringing on pet sitters and dog walkers to lighten your workload. You can hire specialists to help you professionally with business tasks such as marketing, website or graphic design, accounting, and more. You can also hire pet specialists to provide services you'd like to offer your clients, including dog training, cat behavior, and pet grooming.

8. You keep putting off the rest of your life to spend time at work. Before I made radical changes to the way I ran my business, I felt like I was spending more and more time as "Kristin Morrison, Business Owner" instead of simply "Kristin Morrison." Hiring staff will give you time to rekindle the spark for parts of your personal life that have been neglected. You will be giving yourself permission to have passions other than running your business and to nurture relationships and interests outside of your role as a business owner.

9. You are ready to grow your business but can't. If you've had a good idea that you can't find time to implement or have identified a new revenue source but can't give it the time it needs to grow, hire help! You can hire someone to do some of the work you do now, leaving you free to explore new opportunities, or hire someone to work on your new project ... or both.

Now that you know the benefits of hiring (both to you and your business), you are ready to learn everything you need to know to find, hire, and keep the best employees for your pet sitting and dog walking business. But first, take the time to complete this chapter's *Action Steps* to really evaluate the current state of your business.

Kristin's Story:

At one point while running my pet care business, I'd been considering hiring a dog walker to replace me on my dog walks so I could focus on simply managing my business. I'd successfully hired a dog walker to replace me on Tuesdays and Thursdays, but I had been reluctant to give up my Monday/Wednesday/Friday dog walking clients even though I knew I needed to do it. Whenever I am resistant to making a change even though my gut is clearly telling me I need to do it, trouble usually happens... and this was no exception. Trouble happened in the form of a rescue dog named Lyle who I'd been walking for a couple of years with his neighborhood canine friend, Daisy. I picked Lyle up one day for a group hike on a neighborhood trail and left him in my car while I ran into Daisy's house to get her for the hike. When I came back to the car with Daisy (not more than two minutes later), Lyle's mouth was filled with pieces of foam and my back seat was destroyed. I placed a hiring ad for a dog walker the next day and let Lyle and my Monday/Wednesday/Friday dog walking schedule go... and told the new dog walker never to leave Lyle unattended in her car!

Hiring Success Stories:

"I got behind and then felt resentful because I pride myself on my responsiveness to my pet sitting and dog walking clients. I was trying to make the schedule work for my staff and I would pick up all the slack. I was overwhelmed and exhausted and didn't have a life. Now I run an ad on Indeed all the time. I gave all of my pet sitting visits to my employees except for two cat clients. I now have three days to devote to office work! I have a very helpful part-time admin and a tech guy who will be starting soon to get things on the 'to-do list' done."
Robin Lucas - Oak Grove Pet Sitting
Atlanta, Georgia

"I want to expand our pet sitting and dog walking business to different cities, so I'm starting by hiring in those cities and will then start to market and build those areas into our regular service areas."
Heather White Agostini - I've Gone Mutts, LLC
Kennewick, Washington

Action Step

Set your timer for five minutes and answer the following questions in your hiring success journal:

- What big picture items have you been avoiding because you don't have the time or energy to deal with them right now?

- Is there anything you've wanted to do for your business (or have a nagging feeling you should do) that keeps getting postponed because of more urgent deadlines?

Action Step

Set your timer for five minutes. Go back in your hiring success journal and reread the list you made in the *Before You Begin* section of the book of things you would do if you had more time to yourself. Add anything to the list that came to mind as you read through this chapter. Don't hold back! Give yourself permission to really dream big here. This is your chance to visualize the most amazing life and business possible so you have an idea of where you want to go instead of simply focusing on what needs doing today.

Action Step

Set your timer for 15 minutes and answer this next set of questions to get an idea of how hiring exceptional employees will help you better serve your clients:

- How do you react when a client calls or emails? Do you give each response the attention it deserves, or are you shooting back emails on the go between appointments?

- Have you ever lost a client because you simply did not have time for their needs? What happened? What would you have done differently if you'd had more time or more "hands on deck" in your business?

- What do you do now to show your clients that you appreciate their business? What would you like to add or change in the future?

Action Step

Read through the nine signs it's time to hire listed earlier in the chapter. In your journal, write down all the signs that currently apply to you and your business. Put a star next to the two or three signs that are especially frustrating to you or are causing the most difficulties in your business. Next, write down the realizations you had while you read through the list.

Action Step

Mark in your calendar one year from today to review your hiring success journal from beginning to end. If you actively work on the hiring steps contained in this book, starting today and continuing throughout the next few months, you will find your work and personal life have made a complete 180-degree turn!

TWO

How to Hire Confidently

Release Your Fear of Letting Go of Control

"Everything you want is on the other side of fear."

–Jack Canfield

Almost without fail, when a coaching client tells me they are putting off hiring help even after it becomes clear they need it, I can predict the reason: fear. Fear of the quality or reputation of their business declining because their employees might not care as much as they do, fear of letting go of personally providing the pet services and losing touch with what is going on with each client, fear of hiring the wrong person, or fear of overcommitting themselves financially by hiring others to do the work they used to do and burning through all their profits. If you have felt any of these concerns, you are not alone ... but you can't nurture and grow your business from a place of fear. Releasing that fear is the first step to making confident and successful hires.

Why and How Fear is Holding You Back

Fear is normal. In fact, fear is one of the ways your body protects itself from threatening situations. When you encounter physical danger, your brain kicks into overdrive. If you have a fear of heights or are claustrophobic, you know how powerful the body's physical reaction to fear can be. While that desire to avoid risk is completely natural, fear can also keep you from achieving your professional and personal dreams.

Avoiding all risk is not only impossible, but doing so is not good for you or your business. If you were not willing to risk failure, you never would have started your own business in the first place, which means you already have the ability to navigate risk! Trying a new approach to business (for example, offering a new service, expanding your service area, or changing the way you market) can be scary, but it is also the only way to grow past your current limits.

Here are some of the most common fears that prevent entrepreneurs from reaching the next level of growth in their businesses and how to conquer each one:

1. **Fear of uncertainty:** Do you remember how you felt when you first started your business? There was probably a lot of uncertainty about whether you would find enough clients and how much profit (if any) you would actually bring in each month. Uncertainty causes fear because you don't know what to expect or exactly how a situation will play out over time. Oftentimes, your fears are more difficult to handle than the actual problems that arise.

   What you can do about it: The best way to handle fear of uncertainty is to make a solid plan and then take action. How long did it take after starting your business before your uncertainty disappeared? As you experienced each first (your first new client, resolving the first scheduling conflict, filing taxes for the first time), your fear probably diminished as you gained confidence about what to expect.

2. **Fear of failure:** No one wants to fail. Fear of failure can be especially paralyzing if you do not allow yourself space to grow from your mistakes.

   What you can do about it: Instead of thinking of failure as the end, consider what happens next. Give yourself permission to learn from past failures. Thomas Edison famously said, "*I have not failed. I've just found 10,000 ways that won't work.*" Have you had any personal or professional failures that led to a positive outcome in the long run? If you reframe setbacks as a delay on the way to greater success or as

   > THOMAS EDISON FAMOUSLY SAID, "I HAVE NOT FAILED. I'VE JUST FOUND 10,000 WAYS THAT WON'T WORK."

an opportunity for growth, fear of failure will no longer keep you from action.

3. **Fear of rejection:** Pet sitting and dog walking are service-based businesses. So much of what you do as a small business owner is customer service and relationship building. If you are afraid that your customers will react poorly to changes you make (including when you hire someone new), that can hold you back from giving your business what it needs to grow.

What you can do about it: Remind yourself of why your customers picked your business in the first place. Give your clients a chance to show you their loyalty. It takes an incredible amount of trust for someone to let you care for their precious pets. That trust will often extend to those you hire as long as you hire with the same thoughtful consideration that you use when you personally care for pet clients. Most clients would rather give your staff member a try than go through the process of finding a new pet sitter or dog walker anyway.

4. **Fear of change:** Change is not always good, but it isn't always bad either. When you refuse to acknowledge change, you risk getting left behind. Blockbuster Video, Toys "R" Us, and Sears are all examples of one-time household brands that failed to adapt to a changing market.

What you can do about it: The fact of the matter is that change will happen whether you want it to or not. Clients will move away, competitors will join (or leave) your market area, or local regulations may change the way you do business. See the value in change and take control of what you can. Instead of simply waiting for changes to happen to you, initiate the change you'd like to see.

How I Overcame My Fear of Hiring

Before I ever hired my first staff member, I had to overcome my fear of hiring. The first step was becoming aware that I even had a fear of hiring. Because I'd never hired before, I had no idea that it would bring up so many feelings, including fear of a perceived loss of control over my business. If that sounds familiar, you are not alone. I have never worked with a pet business owner who didn't fear putting part of their business in the hands of someone else. This is a very natural reaction, especially if you've carefully nurtured your business from just a thought to an actual business.

Because hiring was such a big step, I couldn't move forward until I recognized that I had such a strong desire to be in charge of every aspect of my business. Even though I would still be in charge of my business, I knew I would be giving up complete control once I let someone else in to help.

One part of overcoming my fear was hiring people I could trust 100% with my clients and my business. I will go over how to do that later in the book. The other part of getting past my fear was recognizing I was afraid and then moving forward in spite of that fear.

I overcame my fear of hiring because I knew I had to if I wanted to create a business that gave me both time and money. I overcame my fear of hiring by simply pushing through the fear, putting one foot in front of the other, and taking the actions needed to hire. I could see that there was one simple reason I needed to hire in order to build the kind of business I wanted: I am only one person. After I'd been in business for a while, I realized I couldn't do it all by myself (nor did I want to!).

Find the Courage to Release Control

It is normal to want to control all aspects of your business. I know I certainly did. A lot of business owners think about their businesses like parents think about their children: they are protective, caring, and thoughtful as they make decisions and changes (as they should be!).

When you've poured so much of yourself into this venture for a few years, you feel an immense sense of ownership and pride in your business. It is scary to relinquish control, but the future of your business depends on it.

Your job, right now at the very beginning of this process, is to face your hiring fear and move forward anyway. It's simply a matter of making the decision to do so and steadily progressing toward your goal of creating a business that can run without you. Even if you're nervous, focus on the signs you listed in your hiring success journal at the end of Chapter 1 that prove it's time to hire. Knowing why you need to hire will help you overcome the natural fear of hiring you may be feeling right now.

Courage is not a coat. You can't just go to a store, buy courage, and put it on. Courage requires going *through* the fear, not around it. You can't just wait for the fear to go away (because it won't). You will find the courage and bravery you need once you go forward anyway, in spite of your fear.

If you are afraid of releasing control of your business (and again, every pet sitter and dog walker I've coached has been afraid of releasing control to some extent), I encourage you to step through that fear. Hiring for the first time will be a little scary, but you do not have to do it alone. I will be sharing the steps you need to take to find and hire the best employees, as well as how to troubleshoot any issues that arise along the way. I will help you cultivate the skills and generate the resources you need to hire with confidence. It will be your job to muster the courage to step through that fear and press onward.

Kristin's Story:

One of the very first staff members I hired was a pet sitter for a client who traveled frequently. This particular client lived in a mansion. I had a lot of fear about whether my new hire, Ingrid, would cause something bad to happen in this expensive home.

The first week Ingrid went to this particular (enormous) home, I was so nervous that I barely slept. I needn't have worried. She ended up doing a great job, and it was such a great reminder of the quote I've heard, "95% of what we're afraid will happen, doesn't". She continued taking great care of that client (and many more of my clients) for years.

Hiring Success Stories:

"So far, I have hired seven people. Terrified, anxious, confused, lost, filled with self-doubt ... that doesn't begin to express how I felt when I first

hired. Every bit of anxiety was worth it! Alleviate your fears by doing your homework. Get your ducks in order even if you don't know how many ducks you should have. Feel the fear AND DO IT ANYWAY!"
Sandy Hafenbrack - Critter Sitters Pet Sitting Service
Yorkville, Illinois

"I definitely had fear during my first hire, but Kristin's coaching helped to give me perspective. My sanity became more important than the fear. The fear mainly stemmed from what clients would say about someone else caring for their pets. My first hire was the perfect fit at the right time, and that experience gave me confidence to rinse and repeat!"
Tomika Bruen - Out for a Walk Pet Sitting & Dog Walking
Los Angeles, California

"I would not have stayed in the pet sitting and dog walking business 28 years without help. I hired my first employee in year six and I wish I had done it sooner. It was scary, but most exciting things in life are! Hiring was what I needed to do to move forward in my business. I love my staff and they allow me to truly have the best of both worlds: work I love and also a lot of personal freedom."
Kim Otone Tank - Apronstrings Pet Sitting, Inc
Pollock Pines, California

Action Step

With your hiring success journal, go back and review the four most common fears business owners have. How many apply to you? Set your timer for five minutes and write about what risks or changes you are afraid to take in your own business. Does the idea of hiring make you nervous? Why? This is your chance to really take a look at what is causing you to feel afraid of hiring.

Action Step

Earlier in the chapter, I shared a quote from Thomas Edison that has inspired many inventors and entrepreneurs to keep trying after experiencing failures of their own. Start a collection of similar quotes in your hiring success journal that you can refer back to when you need motivation. Do an internet search for "quotes about success and failure" for some ideas.

Action Step

Create a concise "statement of courage" you can use to encourage yourself whenever you feel the fear around hiring and releasing control. A successful statement of courage will be two sentences or less, in the present tense, and include your motivation to hire.

For example: *I hire four exceptional employees to care for my clients' pets. This allows me the freedom to grow my business and nurture my personal life outside of my business.*

THREE

Decide How Much Help You Need

Use a Systematic Approach to Evaluate What Your Pet Business Needs

"When you're in a startup, the first 10 people will determine whether the company succeeds or not. Each is 10 percent of the company. So why wouldn't you take as much time as necessary to find all the A-players? If three were not so great, why would you want a company where 30 percent of your people are not so great? A small company depends on great people much more than a big company does."

–Steve Jobs

Before you place your help wanted advertisement and start interviewing potential employees, you need to decide exactly how much help (and what kind) your business really needs. If you hire too many employees, you risk running through all of your profit in staff costs. If you don't hire enough, however, you will still find yourself overworked and overwhelmed. In this chapter, I will show you a step-by-step process to evaluate how much help your business really needs.

Step 1: Track Your Income Streams

Do you know which of your business services brings in the most profit? If not, you should. Tracking your income streams will help you make informed decisions on everything from hiring to marketing. I learned this lesson early on in my own business.

A few years into running my business, I had more clients than I could handle, even with help from staff. Managing my staff members, especially the frequent vacations and sick days of my dog walkers, felt like herding cats. I often felt frustrated with the daily demands of the dog walking service part of my business and was looking for a way to simplify. On a whim, I considered dropping the dog walking service we offered to clients in order to make more time for pet sitting and vacation visits, which seemed easier to manage than midday dog walking.

Fortunately, I've made it a habit to "talk to the numbers" before making any major decisions in my business. Before I stopped our dog walking service altogether, I sat down and evaluated the various streams of income. I discovered that dog walking made up 42% of the annual business revenue! Had I dropped that service impulsively, I would have lost nearly half of my business at once. Instead of dropping the service, I began looking for creative ways to organize dog walking schedules instead, to make the dog walking service easier for me to manage.

If you aren't already tracking individual income streams (dog walking, pet visits, overnight pet sitting, etc.) for your business on a monthly and annual basis, start doing so. You may think that you know which services are the most profitable, but until you have the actual numbers, you may be making decisions based on inaccurate information. Before you can confidently move ahead in your hiring process, it is worth taking the time to accurately evaluate your current income. If you are using a pet sitting and dog walking administration software for your business, it may include the option to categorize income received by type of service. If not, you will need to manually record exactly where your income is coming from.

Be sure to categorize each income stream by the service. How much money has your business made from dog walks each month? What about vacation pet visits or overnight pet sitting in clients' homes? If you already have staff members, be sure to make a separate entry for income from the dog walks/pet visits you've personally done, and the income brought in by your employees.

Start a simple Excel spreadsheet to record income for the last 12 months of business. Your spreadsheet might look something like this, but with all 12 months of the year:

	January	February	March	Total:
Dog Walking	$1,000	$1,250	$1,305	$3,555
Staff	$750	$800	$805	$2,355
Owner	$250	$450	$500	$1,200
Overnight Sitting	$850	$920	$525	$2,295
Staff	$700	$800	$300	$1,800
Owner	$150	$120	$225	$495
Pet Visits	$1,295	$1,550	$995	$3840
Staff	$1,000	$1,250	$800	$3050
Owner	$295	$300	$195	$790
			Yearly Income:	$9,690

Your administration or bookkeeping software might include an automatic report function that will generate a similar spreadsheet like the one in the example above. If so, go ahead and use that as long as it will give you monthly totals and separate income generated by you from the income generated by any staff you currently have working with clients.

Once you have a clear picture of your various sources of business income, it should be easy to see what kind of help you need. Are dog walks a large portion of your income? It may be worth hiring additional dog walkers in order to expand that service. If you make a large part of your revenue with vacation pet visits, however, you may find it more helpful to hire pet sitters with flexible schedules during the times you're more likely to need extra help, such as summertime and holidays.

Step 2: Identify What Kind of Help You Need

Are you looking for full-time employees or part-time help? Some of my business coaching clients do very well with a small number of part-time dog walkers and a handful of back-up walkers when someone calls in sick. I devote an entire chapter to employee classification (independent contractors vs. employees) later in the book, but you should have an idea of what basic time commitment you are looking for from potential hires before listing your first job opening.

Here are some of the most common types of staff members you might want to consider for your business:

Dog Walkers with a Set Schedule:

I found it most helpful to advertise and hire dog walkers for certain days of the week and times of day needed. For example, I would hire one dog walker for Monday, Wednesday, and Friday and another for Tuesday and Thursday. No matter what days they are hired to work, all the dog walkers would work between the hours of 10 am to 3 pm.

This system has many benefits:

- You avoid employee burnout by limiting their schedule to a few days a week with a day off in between each work day. Dog walkers that want to earn more money can always pick up pet sitting jobs or agree to cover shifts for other dog walkers who are sick or on vacation.

- Scheduling new clients is easier when you already know which staff members are working on which days.

- Your clients (both the dogs and their humans) will appreciate the routine of a predictable staff walking schedule. Even if one client is served by two different dog walkers, setting a regular rotation will reassure dogs or clients who might be wary of change.

- You can hire as many or as few walkers as you need for certain time slots. If you know you need more dog walkers for M/W/F at lunchtime, you can advertise accordingly. This will increase your chances of finding the right help the first time around instead of finding out too late that your new staff member is unavailable when you need the most help.

Pet Sitters with a Set Schedule:

Hiring pet sitters with a set schedule has many of the same benefits as with dog walkers. A set schedule allows both you and your pet sitters to know what to expect when it comes to assigning them jobs.

Because the demand for pet sitters tends to fluctuate throughout the year, with most of the appointments falling during popular vacation times, the number of your pet sitting clients may vary more than with dog walking. As a result, you may only need one or two pet sitting staff members at first. When you consider the number of pet sitters you plan to hire, however, calculate the number of hours each week you plan to use each sitter in order to avoid paying overtime (I write more about overtime hours in a later chapter). I find it to be generally less expensive to hire two part-time pet sitters than it will be to hire one pet sitter and pay overtime.

You should already have a good idea of how many pet sitting clients you average each month by the time you evaluate your sources of income and schedule in the *Action Steps* at the end of this chapter. Remember that pet sitters can "job share" clients, with one sitter taking the morning visits and another taking the mid-day or evening visits.

On-Call Pet Sitters/Dog Walkers:

One of the most frustrating parts of managing employees for me was dealing with dog walkers suddenly calling in sick or needing to leave town. I sometimes didn't have enough work to justify hiring an entirely new employee, but I also needed someone to fill in when there was a gap in coverage. On-call pet sitters and dog walkers can help fill that gap.

With on-call employees, you notify them that you may need their help during a certain time period (holidays, for example) and ask them to wait for the call. They agree not to leave town or double book themselves just in case you need their help, but there are restrictions on what you can require of your on-call employees.

I go over more wage and scheduling specifics in later chapters, but here are some basic rules of thumb when it comes to paying on-call employees: In many states, you are not generally required to pay on-call employees unless you actually need them to come in and work, but that may vary based on where you live. Setting restrictions on where they can go, what they can do, and how quickly they must respond when on call increases the likelihood that they will be entitled to some pay. An employee that can use his or her time freely while on call is considered off duty and does not require payment. As with the legal specifics of all employment questions, be sure to check with a local employment lawyer so you will know exactly what is required in your area.

On-call employees offer your business incredible flexibility, but it can sometimes be difficult to keep quality on-call employees for long. The best pet sitters and dog walkers are often looking for something more stable so they can make plans for vacations, childcare, and any other jobs they might have on the side. For more information on covering shifts with existing staff, keep reading. I cover the topic in the chapter on staffing and scheduling.

One solution is to have your regular pet sitters and dog walkers cover last-minute shifts as needed. By doing so, you'll already have trained employees you can trust and give them the chance to make some extra money. The very best solution would be to have the employees themselves arrange to have shifts covered if they need to go out of town or call in sick, although you may have to facilitate this at first to make sure every shift is covered every time. I write more about this in the chapter on scheduling employees later in the book.

Step 3: Make a Schedule

Now that you know which services are bringing in the most income, and you have identified what kind of help you can use, it's time to figure out exactly *when* you need to hire your new staff members. It won't do you any good to hire pet sitters if they plan to travel over the summer and holidays or weekends. You will find a better fit for your company if you can clearly specify the schedule and times you are looking to fill.

What times of day/week/year do you need the most help? This might be your busiest time, or it might be the time of day you'd like to focus on other aspects of the business while employees handle the dog walking and pet sitting for you. For example, if your ideal morning is spent on office work and other professional development, it will be helpful to hire someone to take the morning dog walks or pet visits that you have been handling yourself.

How many more clients could you take on if there were more open hours on the schedule? If you have been turning away business because you are all booked up, what times and days are most often requested? These are the first spots you should look to fill with your new employees.

It is also okay (and sometimes essential) to hire someone so you can take time for yourself. If you've ever flown on a plane with a child, you are familiar with the oxygen mask guidelines: Always fit your own mask before helping the child next to you. Why do airlines have this procedure? It's because you won't be able to help anyone if you don't first help yourself. The same is true in your business. One of the best freedoms that comes from properly staffing your business is the ability to take time off when you need it, whether that means staying home when you're sick, taking a much-needed vacation, or setting aside a few hours each week to nurture your personal relationships or other interests.

> **Hiring Tip:**
> College students can be a great resource for holiday staffing. Many college students return home over the summer and during long holidays and are looking for a way to earn some extra cash without having to commit to a long-term job.

Hiring Holiday-Only Staff

It is not uncommon for pet sitting and dog walking employees to either quit or request time off right during your busiest times of the year. Long holiday weekends, the season from Thanksgiving to New Year's Day, and summer months are times when more people are often looking for someone to care for their pets ... and are the same times that your staff members may be planning vacations of their own. One solution is to hire additional help a couple of months before the busy seasons each year and to ask new and existing staff about their end-of-year holiday availability as early as August or September for the coming holiday season.

College students can be a great resource for holiday staffing. Many college students return home over the summer and during long holidays and are looking for a way to earn some extra cash without having to commit to a long-term job.

I have some coaching clients who use seasonal hiring as an opportunity for identifying the best employees for the remainder of the year. They might only hire new staff for a set period of time around the busy season, for example, but offer the very best employees the chance to stay on at the end of the summer or holidays. This way, they retain only the dog walkers and pet sitters that were the most reliable and took the best care of their clients.

Every Business Has Its Own Needs

In the end, you will only want to hire the number and type of employees that benefit your business. What works for one company may not be a good fit for yours. The information and *Action Steps* in this chapter will help you determine how much help your business needs before you begin searching for the right people to fill those spots.

Kristin's Story:

The first year I hired pet sitters, I learned the hard way the importance of making sure they were available for what are often the busiest times of year in a pet sitting business: Thanksgiving, Christmas, and New Year's.

I neglected to ask my two first hires about their holiday availability and simply assumed they would be available for our busiest time of year. However, in October, when we began getting holiday reservations, both of my new hires said they had holiday plans. At that point, it was too late to hire more pet sitters and so I was stuck scrambling to handle all of the holiday pet sits myself.

After that year, I made a point to always ask applicants about their holiday availability. If they weren't available during the holiday time period, I usually wouldn't hire them. This question is included in the Application Packet for Pet Sitters and Dog Walkers I created (you'll find the link in the *Action Steps*).

From then on, I would always ask new staff about their holiday availability well ahead of time and would get that holiday commitment from them early, which really helped me be prepared for future holiday seasons.

Hiring Success Stories:

"When confirming holiday availability with my staff, I've learned I have to be super clear on exactly which dates I'm referring to and the time of day I need availability. I can have staff say they're available during the holidays but then it sometimes turns out they need Christmas Eve off, which is a huge hole that then needs to be filled by someone else."
Stephanie Surjan - Chicago Urban Pets
Chicago, Illinois

"I think my biggest mistake was not specifying that even though it is a part-time job, my staff cannot have an indefinite amount of days off! I hired someone last year and in less than a year she had taken 256 days off. On top of that, she tried to take every single weekend on next year's calendar and mark herself off! Needless to say, she's no longer working for me."
Josie Hamel - Pets R Us Pet Sitting Services, LLC
Little Elm, Texas

Action Step

Look at your business's dog walking and pet sitting schedule of completed appointments for the past year if you have them. When are your busiest periods? You might notice a day of the week or season of the year where business was really booming.

How many staff members would it take to alleviate the strain during the times that you, or your current staff, are overbooked? Make a sample weekly and monthly schedule that includes the number of additional employees you think you need. Seeing a possible schedule laid out will quickly show you whether or not you have enough work to justify the number of employees you'd like to hire. Adjust the sample schedule as needed until you think you've found the right number of new employees.

Action Step

If you haven't already, make an accurate record of all your income streams for the past 24 months. If you don't have access to a full two years' worth, aim for at least 12 months. Use an automated report from your pet sitting administrative software or manually create a simple Excel spreadsheet as described in this chapter. Customize your spreadsheet so you can clearly see in black and white what services and months net the most income. Information and data are empowering and revealing. Analyzing these numbers will give you a clear picture of your business.

Action Step

Look at your list of income streams. Are there any services you could easily expand if you had more help? Is there a service you'd like to personally do less often but is too lucrative to drop? Identify any services offered currently that you'd like to hand over to someone else or increase by adding more help to the schedule. These are the services you should staff first.

Action Step

What kind of help does your business need? Are you looking for dog walkers, pet sitters, or both? Given how much business you have, do you anticipate needing help all year or only seasonally during your busiest times? In your hiring success journal, make a list of how many staff members you need to cover specific services.

If you still aren't sure what you need, try this exercise for clarity. Set a timer for three minutes and answer the following questions: Which services do you no longer want to provide clients yourself? What services are you, as the business owner, willing to let go of, even if you still enjoy doing them? What days of the week or times of day would you prefer to be "off duty" or free to work on other aspects of your business?

You can find the Application Packet for Pet Sitters and Dog Walkers and other hiring products by going to www.SFPSA.com/petsit. To find out more about the Application Packet specifically, go to this link: www.SFPSA.com/packet.

FOUR

Independent Contractors vs. Employees

Choose the Right Staff Classification Before You Hire

"The misclassification of employees as independent contractors is a nationwide problem that continues to grow and contribute to the tax gap."

–Michael McKenney, Acting Inspector General for Audit in the Department of the Treasury

One of the first decisions you need to make in your hiring journey is what type of workers you will employ. There are four basic ways to engage people in work: directly as an employee, directly as an independent contractor, indirectly as an employee, or indirectly as an independent contractor. Indirect employment means using a staffing company or professional employer organization (PEO) in your hiring process.

While indirectly engaging workers is common in some industries, most pet sitting and dog walking companies hire directly, either by hiring employees or by utilizing independent contractors. These are the two types of workers I will cover in this chapter since almost all pet service businesses use one (or both) of these worker types.

Employee classification is a complicated issue and subject to a variety of statutes and restrictions both on the federal and local levels. I am going to limit this chapter to the IRS federal tax classification because it gives the best general overview of the topic and because many states use federal tax classification as a starting point in any legal disputes over employee classification and compensation.

As always, if you have any questions about the legal or financial implications of classification, check with a local employment lawyer and your accountant. You can find my suggestions for low-cost legal aid in the *Recommended Resources* section. An ounce of prevention really is worth a pound of cure in this case because misclassifying workers can be an incredibly costly mistake.

How to Tell the Difference: Independent Contractor or Employee?

The main differences between independent contractors (ICs) and traditional employees boil down to control. Who is in control of the worker's schedule, actions, and pay? Who decides what steps need to be taken in the process of completing the work? Which party assumes the primary financial risk and opportunity for profit? Workers that are responsible for their own time, work, and billing are usually independent contractors. Workers that rely on their employer for scheduling, assignments, and pay are usually traditional employees.

Every situation is unique, so it can sometimes be confusing to figure out if you should hire (or are already employing) employees or independent contractors. When it comes to settling a dispute or determining tax liability, the IRS and most employment lawyers will evaluate all facets of the work relationship to determine who has control.

In the following table, you will find the differences between ICs and employees in areas like hiring and firing practices, training, and pay. Read through each category to become more familiar with the two classifications before deciding which is best for your business.

Hiring	Independent Contractor (IC)
	The IC often submits a resume and proposal covering the work to be done and the proposed rate. The IC is then given a contract limited to the scope of the work proposed. In cases where an IC submits an application, it is clearly stated that the application is for contract work.
	Employee
	The potential employee submits an application and receives a job offer which details the scope of employment and pay and benefits information.
Pay	Independent Contractor (IC)
	An IC is paid in a number of ways: based on hours of work, by job milestone, or as a lump sum at the completion of the terms of the contract. ICs are paid at the completion of a task or the entire job. ICs generally submit an invoice for work completed. Straight commission pay (without a base salary) is generally an indication of contract work.
	Employee
	Employees are either paid a salary or an hourly rate. Either pay structure can, but does not always, include bonuses or commission-based pay. Employees are also paid on a regular basis, generally weekly, monthly, or twice a month.
Equipment & Supplies	Independent Contractor (IC)
	ICs pay for their own equipment and supplies and are able to count them as tax deductions when they file taxes each year.
	Employee
	The employer pays for equipment or supplies up front or reimburses employees when they need to make a purchase.

Benefits	**Independent Contractor (IC)**
	ICs do not generally have access to any health benefits, retirement plans, or vacation time.
	Employee
	Benefits vary, but employees are generally entitled to some form of group health insurance and vacation time.
Training	**Independent Contractor (IC)**
	ICs are not trained or given a training manual. An independent contractor already has the skills necessary to complete the job. Business owners cannot specify how the work is completed or in what order. Any meetings or communication sharing information about job duties or expectations must be voluntary for the IC and cannot be called "training".
	Employee
	Employees can be taught job duties via paid training, a probationary period, and/or a training manual. An employer is entitled to dictate what work is done, when it is done, *and* how it is completed.
Firing	**Independent Contractor (IC)**
	Business owners cannot "fire" ICs because they are not business employees in the first place. If the IC is not completing work in a timely manner or the work is not meeting the required quality, the contract may be terminated.
	Employee
	Employees who are not meeting an acceptable level of performance may be terminated according to local employment laws.
Tax Forms	**Independent Contractor (IC)**
	An IC receives a 1099 from any employers and uses that to file and pay taxes.
	Employee
	At the end of each tax year, employees are given a W-2 that lists all compensation, wages, and taxes withheld for the year.

Financial Risks	**Independent Contractor (IC)**
	ICs do not depend on an employer to offer their services to the public. That often means they purchase or rent facilities or equipment on their own in order to conduct business. They may advertise and bill clients on their own. They are also allowed to hire their own employees or ICs without the permission of, or even introducing the new employee or IC to the business owner. ICs usually carry their own liability insurance (if required).
	Employee
	Employees do not usually have the ability to offer their goods or services independent of their employer. Employees do not usually advertise independently or incur great financial risk. Clients generally pay the business instead of individual employees.
Worker Protections	**Independent Contractor (IC)**
	True ICs are not covered under many federal employee protection acts, such as the Fair Labor Standards Act (FLSA), National Labor Relations Act (NLRA), or the Employee Retirement Income Securities Act (ERISA). Some non-discrimination laws still apply to ICs. ICs are not eligible for workers' compensation.
	Employee
	Employer/employee interactions are governed by a number of federal regulations as outlined in FLSA, NLRA, and ERISA. Employers may not discriminate against employees who are members of any protected class according to federal law: race, religion, national origin, age, sex, pregnancy, citizenship, familial status, disability, veteran status, or genetic information. Employers are required to provide workers' compensation coverage for employees who are injured at work.

Does it Really Matter?

You may be wondering if it really matters how you classify the staff members you hire. The short answer is *yes, it really matters!*

At its most basic, employee classification is a tax issue, and you absolutely do not want to violate state or federal tax law. Misclassifying employees can cost you thousands of dollars in fines, back taxes, and legal expenses.

If it becomes clear to the IRS or another government agency that you have misclassified employees as independent contractors, you will be required to pay all back taxes and withholdings on top of any applicable fines. At the time of this writing, this includes a minimum of 1.5% of the total federal withholding for the employee's wages, 40% of all FICA taxes (Social Security and Medicare) that were not withheld from that employee's pay, and 100% of the FICA taxes you should have paid as the employer. Interest and penalties are compounded daily from the first date of hire, which can add up to an incredibly expensive mistake!

It is important to know whether you are looking for an independent contractor or a traditional employee *before* you start the hiring process. You want to be very clear in your interview about how each worker will be classified to avoid any misunderstandings in pay and tax responsibility.

The hassle and expense of fixing an error in employee classification will always be worse than simply taking the time to do it right the first time... no matter how much you dread doing paperwork.

That doesn't mean you have to wade through the legal wording alone. Keep reading to find out the pros and cons of each type of classification and how to know which is best for your business.

If you already have staff members that you think may be misclassified, you may qualify for a reduction in back taxes through the IRS's "Voluntary Classification Settlement Program." Check the *Recommended Resources* section for more information.

Deciding Which Type of Worker Your Business Needs

From a business owner's perspective, there are advantages and disadvantages to hiring each type of worker.

Here are some of the most common pros and cons for employees and independent contractors:

Independent Contractor Advantages

- Independent contractors are faster and easier to hire because you are required to submit less paperwork than when hiring a traditional employee.

- ICs have no guarantee of work outside of the contract terms, so you can enlist the help of your IC only when you need it without committing to providing them long-term work.

- You take on less financial commitment and risk with ICs, since they generally carry their own liability insurance and pay their own employment taxes.

Independent Contractor Disadvantages

- If you misclassify an employee as an independent contractor, the fines and back taxes are astronomical.

- You have limited control over the work done, including what steps are taken in the process of completing a job and whether or not they hire others (and who they hire) to assist with the work.

- A contractor's work schedule is very fluid and voluntary. You cannot require them to work a particular weekend if they weren't hired specifically for that weekend and if they don't want to take on the extra work.

From the client's point of view, the freedom afforded independent contractors might not be welcome. How will your clients feel, for example, if a contractor hires staff of their own to complete a visit or walk?

Employee Advantages

- You have more control over how employees represent your business and how they do their job. If you expect employees to complete a certain checklist of duties on a dog walk or pet visit, this control will be a major advantage.

- Staffing and scheduling are simpler because you have control over the hours and days each employee works.

- There is no risk of misclassification because there is no penalty for treating a worker that might qualify as an IC as an employee.

Employee Disadvantages

- You are responsible for all tax withholdings and filings on the state and federal level for each employee. This costs more money and can take time away from your other responsibilities.

- You assume liability for the employee's actions on the job. Their actions and words represent your business and can be used against your business in a legal dispute.

- A large number of employment laws dictate how you interact with employees, and you will need to be sure you are in line with those requirements.

If you still aren't sure which type of worker is the best fit for your business, I recommend using California's new 3-part evaluation tool because it is relatively simple to use. What if you aren't in California? Many states implement California's laws and regulations to make things easier for companies that function in multiple states and because California is home to such a large portion of the country's workers.

California's ABC Evaluation Tool

You must be able to answer "yes" to all three of the following questions in order to classify your workers as independent contractors. If you answer "no" to any of the following questions, you should hire traditional employees.

A: Is the worker free of control and direction of the hiring entity in connection with the performance of work, both under the contract for the performance of work and in fact?

B: Is the worker that performs the work outside the usual course of the hiring entity's business?

C: Is the worker customarily engaged in an independently established trade, occupation, or business?

As you can see from reading through the classification criteria and California's ABCs above, most pet sitters and dog walkers you hire will need to be classified as traditional employees. Not only are they not generally in complete control of what work is done and how (point A), they are also doing work that is part of the regular scope of your business (point B). Although this puts more financial burden on you as the employer, it will enable you to maintain more control over your business and avoid expensive fines and back taxes down the road.

Making Sure You Are in Line with the Law

What if a worker or auditor feels that you are misclassifying workers? In the case of a dispute, a judge will use the primary difference between employees and independent contractors to make a ruling. That difference is control.

Legally, control will be evaluated in three ways: behavioral control (who controls the actions and behavior of the worker), financial control (who bears the financial risk and responsibility), and the relationship between the two parties (repeated business and benefits, for example). The work contract is often used to determine the original intent of the employer and worker as well.

Like I wrote at the beginning of the chapter, employee classification is complicated and varies from state to state. I always recommend meeting with an employment lawyer and your accountant before making any hiring decisions to be sure that your plan is in line with federal and local laws. You will find a list of low-cost employment attorneys in the *Recommended Resources* section.

If you have already hired help and still aren't sure whether you are classifying them correctly after reading this chapter and consulting with an employment lawyer, you can submit a request for the IRS to evaluate your specific situation and officially declare the legal status of your staff members. Be aware that it can take up to six months to get the ruling back from the IRS and completing this request may trigger an audit if you ever try to use or continue to use independent contractors in the future. Most business owners will not need to take this step. Just know that it is an option if you feel your situation is complicated enough that you need an official determination directly from the IRS. I've included a link to the exact form you need in the *Recommended Resources* section at the end of this book.

Kristin's Story:

In the past few years, I've worked with a number of pet sitters and dog walkers who have called me frantic because they misclassified their workers as independent contractors instead of employees. The trigger to the IRS most often happens when independent contractors get "fired" by the company and the ICs try to apply for unemployment. Because they have most recently been independent contractors, they are often unable to get unemployment benefits, and the unemployment office will then contact the state and federal employment agencies to determine whether that particular worker was classified correctly.

There have been a handful of pet sitters and dog walkers that I've worked with who, at least according to them and their local employment attorneys, are using independent contractors in a legal way, but it's rare. It's very important to make sure you've classified correctly and are following all the state and federal guidelines when hiring in order to avoid spending a lot of time, money, and energy in the future to fix the misclassification.

Hiring Success Stories:

"I converted from ICs to employees years ago. I searched online for everything I could to make sure I had all the tax forms I needed, got an account with my state's Employment Development Department, found workers' comp coverage, then told everyone that we were switching from IC to employee. Although I only had two or three people at that point, I explained to them that they would have to take a pay cut due to the conversion. I expected resistance but had absolutely none. In fact, they were thrilled not to have to deal with their own taxes and to know that they were covered by disability and workers' comp. All of them are still with me and it has been seven years since we did this."

Shelly Ross - Tales of the Kitty
San Francisco, California

Action Step

Look through the chart at the beginning of the chapter comparing independent contractors and traditional employees. Make a note in your hiring success journal about whether your employees (or future employees) are more like independent contractors or traditional employees for each category listed.

Action Step

If you already have staff members that you think may be misclassified after reading through the chapter, head to the *Recommended Resources* section at the end of the book for information on the Voluntary Classification Settlement Program to lessen your tax penalty.

Action Step

Using California's ABC evaluation tool described earlier in the chapter, make a decision: Will you be hiring traditional employees or independent contractors? Once you have made a decision, go back and read through the pros and cons of the classification you've chosen. Set your timer for five minutes and make a list in your hiring success journal of the benefits to your business of the hiring classification you've chosen.

Action Step

Consult with a local employment lawyer about what steps you need to take in the hiring process to properly classify your workers. If you need help finding an employment lawyer, do an online search for "low-cost employment lawyer in my area" or check the *Recommended Resources* section for my other recommendations to find inexpensive legal help.

FIVE

Prepare for the Business Side of Hiring

The Paperwork, Insurance, and Savings You Need Before Your Staff Members Start

*"I don't pay good wages because I have a lot of money;
I have a lot of money because I pay good wages."*

–Robert Bosch

One concern for business owners preparing to hire is whether or not they really can afford to pay another (or first) employee. I've occasionally heard from clients that have to let a new staff member go (even when the person has done a great job) because they didn't have all their finances and paperwork in order. This chapter is all about the nuts and bolts of preparing to hire so you don't have any negative surprises a few months in.

Use this chapter to make sure you are prepared in these three ways:

(1) Have the financial means to pay your new staff member's salary,

(2) Get all the types of insurance you will need as an employer, and

(3) File the appropriate paperwork to hire legally.

Budget for Your New Hire

Whether you hire one employee or 10, you will need to be financially prepared to pay for the salary and any applicable taxes and fees for each staff member before you place your first help wanted ad.

So exactly how much money do you need in the bank before you hire? That will depend on how much you plan to pay each staff member and how many people you plan to hire. The first step to determining how much you can afford to pay your employees is to evaluate your current business income and expenses.

If you've made it this far in your business without separating your personal and business finances, now is the time to make the change and separate your financials. Once you start paying staff in addition to business expenses and your own salary, it will be more important than ever to be organized and intentional with your finances.

I am going to show you an easy way to track your income and expenses with a spreadsheet, but you can also use budgeting software to simplify the process. If you need ideas, you can find accounting software recommendations in the *Recommended Resources* section in the back of the book.

If you already have a dedicated bank account for your business and a business budget software that tracks your income and expenses each month, you may want to skip to the next section for information on how to determine what you can afford to pay your new employee(s).

The most basic way to maintain a business budget is to start with a list of all your anticipated expenses each month. Then throughout the month, record the actual costs in a separate column to get a running total of money spent that month.

	ESTIMATE	ACTUAL
Accounting		
Advertising: online		
Advertising: print		
Advertising: miscellaneous		
Auto insurance (work car)		
Auto maintenance (work car)		
Auto payment (work car)		
Bank charges		
Computer		
Contracted work		
Equipment		
Gas		
Insurance: business		
Licenses		
Membership fees		
Office supplies		
Parking fees and tolls		
Pet supplies		
Phone		
Salary (me)		
Salary (staff)		
Tax payments		
Utilities		
Website		
TOTAL BUSINESS EXPENSES:		

Combined with the income streams you tracked in Chapter 3, you will have all the information you need to determine how much money you can use for staff compensation each month.

Determine How Much You Can Afford to Pay

By subtracting your total expenses from your total monthly income, you will have a clear picture of each month's profit. Some of this money will go toward paying your staff, but even while paying staff salaries, it's very important to set aside money for savings each month out of this profit—both for future business expenses and for your personal future.

I regularly advise new pet business owners to set aside money each month into a "saving for the future" fund. I once had a coaching client tell me that her number one goal was one I hear a lot: to save enough money to quit her day job and run her business full time. Together, we brainstormed names for her savings account that would inspire her while she worked toward that goal. She ended up naming it "My New Life Account", and I've been encouraging clients to pick inspiring names for their savings accounts ever since.

If you know you plan to hire help for your business, but aren't ready to take that step immediately, start setting aside savings specifically for hiring. That way, when you are ready to make that first hire, you already have a small nest egg to pay for getting your new staff member hired, insured, and trained.

Once you've calculated your average monthly profit and deducted your monthly savings, you can accurately calculate how much money you have to pay future staff. Use that number to set a realistic estimate of how many hours you can pay someone to work each month. If the pay you have available doesn't match the number of employees you calculated that you need in Chapter 3, you will need to find more money in the budget by either making more money, lowering other expenses, or reducing the number of employees you hire (or hours you offer) at first.

When you initially make a hire, you will likely experience a financial dip because you're effectively giving some of your business and income away to your new staff member. What ends up happening then is that you create a vacuum in your business, allowing you to have more time and space to take on new clients, up your marketing game, and attract even more clients.

Trust me when I say that the time and energy initially spent on hiring will be worth it. You may find that you replace that lost income with even more ... not to mention the non-monetary benefits of hiring, such as more time and freedom for you as the business owner. When you have time to really nurture your business and nourish yourself, which happens when you start hiring, you will be able to create more prosperity and peace.

> WHEN YOU HAVE TIME TO REALLY NURTURE YOUR BUSINESS AND NOURISH YOURSELF, WHICH HAPPENS WHEN YOU START HIRING, YOU WILL BE ABLE TO CREATE MORE PROSPERITY AND PEACE.

Insurance for Your Staff and Your Business

In addition to the personal and business insurance policies that you currently have, you will need to make some additions once you start hiring employees.

Workers' compensation insurance: Each state has its own workers' compensation requirements, but you should expect to purchase an insurance policy to cover each employee in case of injury or illness due to a workplace accident. Some states only require employers to carry insurance once they have a certain number of employees, and that number will vary from state to state. You can often purchase workers' compensation insurance through the company that provides your current business insurance, so start your quote gathering there.

Bonding (anti-theft) and pet business insurance: You are likely already bonded and insured, as doing so gives your clients peace of mind and gives you certain protections against risk and litigation. It is not very expensive to bond and insure your employees as well, and it's absolutely crucial that you do so. Contact your current insurance carrier to find out how to add new staff members to your policy.

Health insurance: Health insurance benefits are an expensive addition to your expenses each month but can also be a major attraction to potential job applicants. Under current federal law, employers with fewer than 50 full-time employees are not required to provide health insurance coverage to their employees, so you will probably not need to budget for this expense. Laws can and do change, however, so definitely check with an employment attorney to find out what the legal requirements are in your particular state.

If you do want to offer some sort of group plan to your employees, I recommend you visit the Small Business Health Options Program (SHOP) website to compare current options, prices, and available tax credits.

If you don't currently have an insurance company you are satisfied with, or are planning to shop around to compare rates, send me an email at Success@SFPSA.com for my recommendations.

Tax Paperwork and Record Keeping for Employees

Immediately after you hire a new employee, there are a number of forms that you will need to file with state and federal tax agencies. If you don't have one already, you will need to apply for an Employer Identification Number (EIN). The easiest way to obtain an EIN is by applying online at IRS.gov. You only need to do this once, no matter how many employees you eventually hire. Some states also require you to obtain a similar identification number from the state. In California, for example, employers need to register with the Employment Development Department before paying staff members.

On or before their first day, each employee will need to fill out the following: IRS Form W-4 and section one of IRS Form I-9. The I-9 form includes their basic contact information and eligibility to work in the United States. Legally, you are required to keep the I-9 on file for three years after the date of hire or a full year after their termination, whichever is later. The W-4 is used to determine how much federal and state tax to withhold from each paycheck, so be sure to keep a copy of this form on file as long as they work for your business.

An important legal distinction you'll need to know is the difference between exempt and nonexempt employees. In most cases, the determination is made based on three criteria: how much they are paid, how they are paid, and what kind of work they do.

- **How much they are paid:** According to federal law, exempt employees must meet a minimum pay requirement (set by the current Fair Labor Standards Act). Your state may have a higher minimum.

- **How they are paid:** Exempt employees are paid a set salary (as opposed to an hourly or per-piece rate, which I explain in further detail in the chapter on paying staff), but that is not a cut and dry test, as some nonexempt employees are paid a set salary.

- **What kind of work they do:** In addition to the minimum pay and salary pay, exempt employees must also be engaged in executive, administrative, or highly specialized duties for at least 50% of the time worked. Highly specialized work is limited to duties that require a high level of education and licensing to complete, such as the work performed by attorneys, professors, and therapists. In the case of administrative work, you must be able to clearly show that the job duties involve the exercise of independent judgment about decisions with a significant impact on the business. Regular office assistant work (answering phones, filing paperwork) does not qualify, nor does the pet care (walking dogs, pet visits) provided by your business.

Nonexempt employees are entitled to overtime pay, while exempt employees are not. You may read that and think you'd prefer to have exempt employees, but the law is very strict on what qualifies as an exempt employee to prevent employers from taking advantage of the system to avoid overtime pay.

Almost all staff members in a pet sitting and dog walking business will be nonexempt. If you are at all unclear about whether or not an employee qualifies as exempt, err on the side of caution and classify them as nonexempt. Doing so significantly mitigates your legal risk. You can also contact a local employment lawyer if you have any doubts about employee classification. Check the *Recommended Resources* section for options for low-cost legal aid recommendations.

In addition to tax documentation, the Department of Labor requires employers to maintain an accurate record of the following items for each nonexempt employee throughout the entire length of employment:

1. Employee's full name and Social Security number

2. Mailing address (including the ZIP code)

3. Birth date, if younger than 19

4. Sex

5. Occupation

6. Day and time when the employee's workweek begins

7. Hours worked each day

8. Total hours worked each workweek

9. Basis on which employee's wages are paid (rate per hour, per-piece, etc.)

10. Regular hourly pay rate

11. Total regular earnings for each week worked

12. Total overtime earnings for each week worked

13. Deductions and additions to employee's wages

14. Total wages paid in each pay period

15. The pay period and date of payment of each payment

As you can see from the list, organization will be so important once you start hiring. The good news is that you will not need fourteen separate documents for these records; most of this information can be tracked through the initial hiring paperwork and regular pay statements.

What about employees that work irregular hours from week to week? Again, much of what you need to keep track of will be recorded on your wage statements already. All you need to do to meet the requirements for items 6, 7, and 8 is to accurately track when they work and when each pay period starts and ends.

One important note on wage statements: Be aware that it really does matter what information is and isn't listed on your wage statements. Some states, including California, have very specific requirements for what must be on each wage statement, and failing to comply can be a costly mistake.

Important Dates to Remember

As an employer, there are certain dates you need to be aware of each year. These dates are set by federal and state agencies and are subject to change. Definitely verify with your local authorities to make sure these dates are applicable in your area.

Within 20 days of a new hire: File a New Hire Report to your state employment agency. Many states offer electronic reporting. Do an internet search for "new hire reporting in (your state)" to find out what your state requires.

January 31: By the end of January, you must submit a Form W-2 to the IRS, either electronically or with a paper copy of the form, for each employee that worked for you the previous year.

If you hired independent contractors the previous year, you must also submit a Form 1099 for each IC if their pay qualifies as "non-employee compensation" (box 7). Check with an accountant if you have any question about whether your situation qualifies.

Your quarterly federal tax return and FUTA (Federal Unemployment Tax Act) Form 940 are due for the previous quarter.

March 31: 1099s that do not include non-employee compensation (box 7) are due to the IRS. Again, consult a qualified accountant for help determining which deadline applies if your company used independent contractors in the previous year.

April 30: Your quarterly federal tax return and Form 940 are due for the previous quarter.

July 31: Your quarterly federal tax return and Form 940 are due for the previous quarter.

October 31: Your quarterly federal tax return and Form 940 are due for the previous quarter.

If all of these dates and forms are making your head spin, take a deep breath. Payroll software and a knowledgeable accountant can help you with any questions you have along the way.

Kristin's Story:

I've coached a number of pet sitters and dog walkers who wanted to hire but were afraid to for financial reasons. I also experienced that fear before my first hire. It was a risk to let go of some of the work (and pay) I'd been receiving and to give it to a staff member instead.

For me, and for those I've coached, there often is a period of financial fear and insecurity after hiring the first few staff members. However, that is often quickly replaced by a sense of freedom and excitement at having more time to work ON the business instead of IN the business.

If you've crunched the numbers like I wrote about in this chapter, and it makes sense for you to hire (even if it's a bit of a stretch financially), I highly recommend that you do it because it will give you more time and energy to build your business. As a result, you'll have more time and money than you ever did before hiring. Remember: there's only so much of you to go around in your business!

Hiring Success Stories:

"I was very anxious to hire but I just kept in mind that: a) this was what I needed and wanted for the growth of my business, and b) other people have hired successfully, so I could, too. Other than a couple staff members that were not so great, most have been great hires, and I would hire them again if they needed a job! The important takeaway from the not-so-great hires is that it helps you learn what traits in people are red flags and what you want to avoid with the next hire. Also, in every employee mistake made, I can always find something I neglected to do that caused the mistake, or something I could have done to avoid the mistake. Hiring is a learning process!"

Stephanie Sorensen - Zen Dog, LLC
Peachtree Corners, Georgia

"I realized quickly that to be a reliable and dependable pet care business, I couldn't do it alone. Life can be unpredictable; things can happen: car issues, car accidents, injuries or sickness, a family member's illness or death. All of these have happened during my last thirty years of pet sitting. I also feel it's very important to take time off for yourself to be with friends and family. I'm thankful for all of my pet sitters. Two have been with me for over 10 years. My clients feel confident in our care because they know that in case of an emergency another pet sitter can fill in and, because we have a number of sitters, we can be much more flexible, accommodating and rarely have to say no to any of our clients."
Nancy Meller Carlson - Critter Sitter Pet Care
Fuquay-Varina, North Carolina

Action Step

Using your monthly budget and income records, calculate your total profit for the past month. Repeat the process to get three-, six-, and twelve-month totals so you can look at the overall trend. Record these numbers in your hiring success journal along with answers to the following questions: (1) Are my profits going up, down, or remaining steady over the course of a year? (2) What patterns can I see in my spending or earnings that I would like to change? (3) What expense areas can I reduce in order to pay for my new hire(s)?

If you aren't budgeting and keeping track of all the money you spend each month, start this month. Your business will thank you for it.

Action Step

Crunch the numbers. Compare the profits you calculated in the previous Action Step with the number of staff members you plan to hire. If you don't have enough money to pay all of those employees, make a decision: Will you find more money in the budget by reducing expenses or by hiring fewer staff members (or for fewer hours)?

Action Step

Contact your insurance company about anti-theft insurance (bonding insurance), workers' compensation insurance, and adding staff members to your existing business insurance policy. You do not need to pay for either until after you make a hire, but your insurance agent can give you a price quote and let you know what sort of information is needed (and when) to make the policy effective.

If you'd like to check pricing for business insurance through an association, email me at Success@SFPSA.com and I'll give you the name of the association I recommend, as well as a suggestion for business insurance if you do not go through an association.

Action Step

Prepare yourself for the paperwork side of hiring. If you haven't already, apply for an EIN online at www.irs.gov. If your state requires a separate employer registration process (such as the EDD number in California), apply for that as well. Set up a record-keeping system for each employee file. Download any tax forms you need at www.irs.gov/forms.

SIX

Pay Your Staff

How, What, and When to Pay Your Employees

"It stands to reason: higher wages mean higher loyalty and morale, which means higher productivity, which means a more profitable business."

–Thomas Perez

Your job posting and application packet will both include details on pay, so it makes sense to decide how much to pay your employees *before* you start looking for them. I'm focusing on employees in this chapter instead of independent contractors because the vast majority (if not all) of pet sitters and dog walkers you hire will need to be traditional employees. If you use independent contractors in your company (either with or without traditional employees), just know that many of the regulations discussed in this chapter only apply to traditional employees.

Know the Legal Requirements First

First and foremost, it is crucial that you meet all federal, state, and local pay requirements for your employees or independent contractors. Employees, for example, must be paid for all hours worked, including training and time spent meeting new clients. You will find ideas on how to pay employees for client meet-and-greets at the end of this chapter.

Whether you pay by the hour or by the job (which you will learn more about later in the chapter), the cumulative rate of pay will still need to meet or surpass the minimum wage in your area. For that reason, the first step to setting any pay schedule is to know the minimum pay requirement in your city and state.

You can find the federal and state minimum wage laws on the U.S. Department of Labor website at www.dol.gov/whd/minwage. In cases where your state's minimum wage differs from the federal minimum, you will be required to pay whichever is the higher of the two rates:

- If your state's minimum wage is lower than the federal rate, or if your state has no set minimum wage, you will be required to meet the federal rate.

- If your state's minimum wage is higher than the federal rate, you will need to pay enough to meet that higher rate set by your state.

Some cities, especially major urban centers, have citywide minimum wage laws as well. The same principle applies with citywide minimum wages: you must pay the higher of the rates, whether that's the citywide wage, the state wage, or the federal wage.

Those of you in California, like I am, are probably already aware that California has some of the most detailed wage laws in the country. Other states have their own unique wage requirements. To help my coaching clients navigate the legal side of staffing and pay, I have a number of hiring webinar recordings for pet sitters and dog walkers available for purchase on my website. Some of these recordings talk specifically about wage laws. You can find all my hiring webinar recordings and forms available for purchase at www.SFPSA.com/hire.

Ultimately, no matter where you are located, you will want to talk to an employment lawyer licensed to practice in your area to be sure that your business is operating within the legal requirements.

Research What Your Competition is Paying

Finding the right pay rate is critical if you want to attract and keep the best employees. If you pay too little, you risk losing the best staff members to other companies or jobs. If you pay too much, you will cut into the money you need to keep your business profitable. Because prices and pay vary so much by location, I recommend starting with some market research to figure out what the competition is paying their pet sitters and dog walkers.

Go to the job listings on Craigslist and Indeed to see what other pet sitters and dog walkers in your area are paying for walks and sits. If you're part of a local pet sitting and dog walking networking group, ask pet care providers in that group what they are paying their staff. You can also call local pet sitting and dog walking companies that you don't yet know and ask them if they would be open to sharing how much they pay their staff. Some may not want to share this information, but it is still worth trying, especially if you haven't been able to find this information from online help wanted ads or local pet care providers you already know. Make sure to create a spreadsheet to record the rates as you find them so you can clearly see the pay scales of your fellow pet care providers.

The more information you can gather, the more accurate your comparison will be. Record what other businesses are paying their employees per hour or per piece (walk, visit, etc.). I recommend finding the rates of five to seven local businesses that are the most similar to yours if possible. If you aren't sure which businesses are the most similar to yours, look for both businesses that operate in the closest location to yours and those that offer the most comparable services to clients at similar fees to clients.

If there are any companies paying their employees a lot more or less than the average pay rate in your area, try to figure out why. For example, are the rates they charge their clients considerably higher or lower than yours? That could account for the pay differential. When you look at the businesses with the highest employee pay, what sets them apart? Are their employees better trained, more experienced, or certified in pet CPR or another modality? If so, that would allow the company to charge more money (and pay a higher wage as a result).

Your target pay rate should be near the top for your area. Essentially, I recommend you pay your staff as close to the highest rate in your area as possible to attract the very top candidates. Employee satisfaction is not all about money, but having a competitive pay structure will help you keep the best employees loyal to your company.

Establish a Pay Structure: Hourly or Per Piece?

Some business owners prefer to pay employees an hourly rate, while others pay a flat fee per service. When paying hourly employees, you will set a rate for your employees and pay them that rate times hours worked every pay period. For example, if you have a dog walker that works six hours each week, that staff member will earn six times their hourly rate.

You may also want to increase the hourly rate for certain jobs or handling multiple animals at once. Consider adding a flat increase of around 5% for each additional animal on a walk or visit. That way, you are rewarding them for their extra efforts while still staying within an hourly structure.

With per-piece pay, I recommend paying your employees 50% of what you charge a client. That means that for a $20 walk, your employee would be paid $10. Some business owners find this to be a much simpler way to pay employees because it makes their accounting easier. They know that 50% of any client fee goes to the employee and the other 50% goes to business overhead and profit. But as I've stated earlier, some cities and states do not allow per-piece pay, so definitely talk to a local accountant and/or employment attorney if you want to pay your employees this way.

One question I often get is how to pay employees for overnight pet visits. Should they be paid for the entire visit, including the time spent sleeping? Even if you pay your employees per piece, their total pay must at least meet the minimum wage requirement for the hours they work, so how do you factor overnight visits into that pay structure? According to the Fair Labor Standards Act, it depends on how long the employee is at work.

For example, in some states, employees on 24-hour shifts do not need to be paid for sleeping hours, and that law allows you to deduct

Hiring Tip:
Sit down and crunch the numbers to compare paying your employees minimum wage versus paying them 50% of what each service costs. Depending on the minimum wage laws in your area, you may actually find that the pay rates are very similar.

up to 8 hours from each 24-hour shift for sleep. For work that takes fewer than 24 hours (a 7 pm – 7 am overnight visit, for example), the employee must be paid for every hour of the shift, even if some of it was spent sleeping. That means that you, as the business owner, will have to set the schedules and pay that work best for your clients and business within those legal parameters. Again, this is something you will *absolutely* want to clear with an employment lawyer since laws and local regulations vary and are subject to change.

Sit down and crunch the numbers to compare paying your employees minimum wage versus paying them 50% of what each service costs. Depending on the minimum wage laws in your area, you may actually find that the pay rates are very similar.

Giving Raises (and Raising Rates)

I recommend utilizing a tiered structure when it comes to paying your staff members — the longer they've been working for you, the more money they make. The trick is finding the right starting wage and making sure you are bringing in more every year to cover the increase in pay.

I used a three-tiered pay rate for my hourly employees and had great success with it. For the first three months, which I considered a training and probationary period, I paid minimum wage. After the probationary period, I increased their pay by $1/hour. A year later, it went up $2/hour more. Every year after that, I would give them a slight raise, which was paid for by increases in my client fees.

If you haven't increased your prices in a while, or if you need suggestions on the best ways to notify your clients of the price increase, you will find a sample rate increase email template at the bottom of the "Free Stuff" page of my website: www.SFPSA.com/free.

Holiday and Overtime Pay

If at all possible, you will want to avoid paying overtime. It is so much more expensive to pay someone time and a half (or more!) than it is to fill those appointments with other staff members. This is especially important to keep in mind with overnight pet visits and weekend or holiday pet sitting appointments. Anytime an employee works more than forty hours in a week, even if some of those hours are spent sleeping, you will be on the hook for overtime pay.

Some states have additional overtime regulations that are even stricter than the federal ones. In California, for example, employees are entitled to overtime pay if they work more than seven days in a row and for any hours they work over eight hours in a single day, even if they still work under forty hours that week.

Another overtime issue that catches some business owners off guard is that you need to factor nondiscretionary bonuses (any bonus, commission, or incentive tied directly to performance) into the base pay rate used to calculate the overtime rate. Figuring out the correct pay rate for overtime gets complicated quickly, which is another reason I suggest that you avoid overtime if you can. (This is yet another motivation to figure out what is legally required in your area *before* you make a hire.) Don't get hit with costly penalties simply because you failed to investigate the overtime laws in your area.

When it comes to holidays, however, you may have more flexibility on whether or not to pay a higher rate. Under federal law, business owners are not required to pay employees any more on a holiday than they would for a regular shift. As with overtime, your state may have additional regulations or laws around holiday pay.

Even if your state does not require you to pay employees extra for worked holidays, I have always found the boost in employee loyalty and morale to be worth the cost of paying a little bit more than the "going rate". I liked to show my employees that I valued their time, especially during busy holidays.

Here is an idea of what your holiday pay schedule might look like, based on what I did for many years in my own business:

Rather than deal with lots of individual holiday schedules, our main holiday season covered the holidays from November through the first of the year.

- Thanksgiving was a four-day holiday (Thursday-Sunday). Christmas and New Year's were rolled into one end-of-year holiday period that ran from just before Christmas through the first weekend in January. You may also want to consider adding holidays like Hanukkah and Kwanza to your designated holiday schedule.

- During any holiday period, I charged clients 20% extra for each walk or visit. I would split that extra holiday charge with the staff member who covered the shifts. This allowed the business to take in a little extra and for the staff to earn a holiday bonus.

- Most holiday appointments were for pet visits, as most pet owners did not need us to walk their dogs when they were off work for the holiday. When holiday dog walking was needed, however, I applied the regular holiday fee of 20% that I mentioned earlier.

- As with all pay decisions, sit down with your accountant and evaluate what you need to bring in, and what you need to pay out, in order to be profitable and keep the best staff happy to work for you.

Kristin's Story:

I coach a lot of pet business owners who invariably ask me about client meet-and-greets (also known as "client interviews"). These are meetings where pet sitters and/or the business owner meets the pets (and the pets' humans) and become familiar with the house before establishing a working relationship. The pet business owners want to know how best to compensate staff for what is ordinarily a free service offered by most pet sitting and dog walking companies. If you have walkers and sitters who are doing those meetings, they do need to be financially compensated.

There are various ways to compensate them. One way to compensate is to pay staff for their time without charging the client, simply absorbing the pay into the cost of running your business.

Another option is to charge the client a certain amount for the meet-and-greet, pay your staff member for their time from that fee, and then deduct the fee from the client's total pet sitting or dog walking bill. (When you're booking the client interview, let the client know that they will be charged for the meet-and-greet, but that the fee will be credited toward their upcoming bill unless they cancel their pet care needs after the meeting.)

Regardless of which route you take, be sure to let the client know the time amount for a meet-and-greet is thirty minutes or less and any longer than that will be billed in 15-minute increments at X amount. Make sure your staff members know to keep track of the time they are at the client interview and to give a five-minute warning if the thirty-minute deadline is approaching. For example, "I just want to let you know that we have five more minutes. Do you need me to stay beyond that for a small fee?'"

Hiring Success Stories:

"I look at what one needs to make in a month to reasonably get by in my area and determine pay from that perspective. I check the hourly rate from several angles to make sure it's fair for the employee and fair for me: How much revenue are they generating per hour? What are my expenses per hour? What's the profit I want to make? etc. If the revenue the position brings in isn't covering the wage I came up with in step one, I go back to the drawing board. But the question of 'is this a living wage' is always my no exceptions criteria."
Jennifer Bauer - Good Boy Dog Training
Edmonton, Alberta, Canada

Action Step

Learn what minimum pay laws are in effect in your city and state. Do an internet search for your state's minimum wage. An internet search for "minimum wage in (your city)" should tell you if your city has a separate minimum wage. You will find federal and state minimum wage laws at: www.dol.gov/whd/minwage. Consult a local employment attorney if you're uncertain what is the legally required amount to pay your employees.

Action Step

Using the steps outlined in the section "Research What Your Competition is Paying," calculate the average hourly pay for pet sitters and dog walkers in your area. After evaluating the spreadsheet you created, set a rate for your employees. Aim to be in the top 10% for pay in your area.

Action Step

Establish a three-tiered pay structure for new and existing employees. Remember, the longer an employee has been working for you, the more they should be making.

If you currently have employees, increase their pay as needed to fit within the appropriate pay tier.

Action Step

If you haven't increased your prices in a year or more, now is the time to do so. By raising your rates just $1-2 per walk or visit each year, you will increase your annual profits enough to reward your employees with a small raise each year as well. Head to www.SFPSA.com/free for a free rate increase email template (found at the bottom of that page) along with more information on why you should be raising your rates every one to two years.

SEVEN

Harness the Power of an Application Packet

Use the Right Application Process to Help You Find the Best Staff

"You're not just recruiting employees, but are sowing the seeds of your reputation."

–Kirby Smart

Before you ever post a single help wanted ad, it's important to have a plan for screening candidates. Why wouldn't you want to just evaluate each response individually as they come in? Here's why: If all goes well with your advertisement, responses may start coming in faster than you can read them. I've worked with a number of coaching clients who have received over 200 emails over the course of a week or two in response to one help wanted ad!

Even after you've narrowed down the responses to those that could be a good fit for your company, you may still have more quality applicants than you need. Even if you only get 20 promising responses, there is no way for you to interview that many candidates, nor should you. As a small business owner, your time is valuable and limited. This is where the application packet comes in: It will save you more time and energy than you can even imagine.

How My Application Packet Came to Be

Before I detail exactly what is included in an application packet and how you can use it to hire the best employees for your business, let me explain how (and why) I came up with the idea so you can understand why an application packet can improve your current and/or future hiring system.

My early hiring experiences were hit or miss. I had hired a few really wonderful people, but some others had not worked out at all. One woman that I hired ended up taking the dog she was walking to the county fair and feeding it so many hotdogs that it got sick. Thankfully, the client was my good friend and the dog recovered, so we were able to work it out, but the whole situation was a mess. After a few bad hires, I started to doubt my ability to pick the best applicant for the job. I felt like I had to come up with a better hiring solution or stop hiring altogether.

I felt like my hiring "picker" was inconsistent. Sometimes it was "on", and when it was, I would hire someone really great who would stay with my company for years and do a fantastic job. But when my picker was "off", I would make a bad hire, which led to a lot of stress and put my business reputation at risk.

Often this would happen during a very busy time for my business … that's why I was hiring help, after all. I really needed to hire more staff, but I definitely did not have time to interview and train another person that was going to end up being a bad fit for my company. I needed to find a way to develop a more reliable hiring "picker" and to choose the best people who would be great for my business right from the start.

One day, when I was wishing that I had an assistant whose only job was to sift through applications, I had an epiphany. I realized I didn't actually want to hire someone else to do the hiring since I wanted to personally select employees that had the qualities important to me, but I could create a *paper or online document assistant* to do some of that for me. That way, I would be able to spend less time interviewing and more quickly find quality staff members.

After giving the idea some serious thought, I decided to create a "hiring assistant" in the form of a document that would help strengthen my picker. I designed a lengthy and detailed application packet that required a high level of commitment from each potential employee and would enable me to quickly see if they were the right fit before I'd even talked to them! My packet was seven pages long and took a lot of time and effort to fill out. Because it was so detailed, not everyone was willing to complete the whole packet. As a result, the application packet did much of the initial screening for me and saved me countless hours and a whole lot of energy.

If you want to save a lot of time and energy, you can purchase the Application Packet right now and receive it in less than thirty seconds after ordering by going here: www.SFPSA.com/packet. The packet is fully editable so you can easily customize it for your own business.

However, if you want to create an application packet from scratch, that's fine, too — I'll tell you how to do that right now!

Creating Your Own Application Packet

The best application packet is one that helps you figure out which applicants are best for *your* business. For that reason, your packet will not look exactly like any other.

You may choose to add more questions to your packet to fit with your business model, but here is a list of the basic page components I suggest you include to narrow down your pool of candidates:

- **A cover sheet.** This should include return directions so the applicants know where to send the packet when they have completed it and by what date to send it back to you.

- **Job descriptions and starting pay rates for each job.** The packet available for purchase on my website includes separate descriptions and pay rates for three jobs: dog walker, overnight pet sitter, and am/pm pet visitor.

- **A basic job application.** This should include necessary information about the applicant (such as name, phone, address, references, etc.).

- **An application specific to dog walking and / or pet sitting with pet care-related questions.** If you use open-ended questions here, it can save you time in the interview process as well. (More on interview questions in the upcoming chapter on interviewing candidates.)

- **A dog walk schedule and available geographical areas.** This is where the applicant fills out time slots available for dog walks. This will enable you to see at a glance if a particular applicant is available during the days and times you need coverage. This section also lists the cities where you provide service so the applicant can mark the areas in which they are available to provide care.

- **A pet sitter schedule.** Like the dog walking schedule, this will let you see what days the applicant is available for pet sitting. Be sure to include holidays and weekends in this section so you can quickly determine which applicants can cover the days and times you most need help.

- **A questionnaire.** Include questions about how many hours and how much money they are hoping to earn each week from pet sitting or dog walking. I also recommend including a question or two that can help you evaluate how well applicants follow directions. For example, the Application Packet I offer on my website has the following: "List three words that best describe why you would make a great pet sitter or dog walker." If you review that section and see that an applicant has written three sentences instead of three words, you will know right away they are not a good fit. Why? Clients often leave detailed notes to pet care providers, and not following those instructions can be problematic or, even worse, can cause illness or death to a pet.

Be careful not to include any discriminatory language in your job application or packet. If there is any question as to what qualifies as discrimination, check with an employment lawyer or the Equal Employment Opportunity Commission's website (www.eeoc.gov) under the Employers/Small Business tab.

How to Use Your Application Packet

Once you've published a "help wanted" ad and narrowed down your responses to the most likely candidates, email a copy of your application packet to each candidate with instructions to fill out the application and return it to you in whichever method you prefer (snail mail or email).

Here are two sample email templates you can use to create your own standard responses: one for candidates who you can immediately tell are not a good fit for your business and one for the best candidates you'd like to fill out and return an application packet.

For applicants that are not a good fit:

Dear _____,

Thank you for your interest in the [Job Title] position at [Your Company Name Here] and the time you spent applying.

We have selected a candidate and will not be hiring any additional staff members at this time.

Thank you again for your interest.

Best,

[Your Name Here]

For the most promising applicants (to accompany the application packet):

Dear _____,

Thank you for your interest in the [Job Title] position at [Your Company Name Here].

We were very impressed with your qualifications and would like to learn more about how you might be a good fit for our company. Please fill out the attached application packet and return it to [Return Address Here, either email or business mailing address] by [Date Here, usually 5-7 days from when you send the email].

After we receive and review your packet, we will contact you to let you know if you have been selected for an interview.

Thank you again for your interest. Again, we look forward to receiving your packet back by [Date Here] so we can consider you for our in-person interviews, which are happening soon.

Best,

[Your Name Here]

In this chapter's *Action Steps*, you will modify these sample emails to make your own. The first email can be nothing more than a very brief, "No, thank you", but it is incredibly important and polite to respond if you can (as long as you haven't gotten hundreds of responses, of course). You can also use this email as a starting point for any applicants that you send the application packet to but then decide not to interview, though you will want to make it more personal for applicants who took the time to fill out the lengthy packet.

The second email should include instructions on how to fill out the packet, where to send it when it is complete, and how soon you need it back.

Some business owners specifically ask that applicants snail mail back the application packet as a way to evaluate which candidates are willing to work harder and go the extra mile for this job. That dedication can sometimes translate to a better employee overall.

Can candidates email the packet back instead? Sure. I have some coaching clients that prefer to use email exclusively, often as a way of saving time. That really is your decision to make based on your schedule and hiring priorities.

Review the packets as they start coming back and decide which applicants really stand out. Call the best candidates for an interview (I write more about how to conduct an effective face-to-face interview in another chapter).

Another benefit of the application packet is that it will save you valuable time. Your experience may vary, but I typically received about 50% of the packets back that I sent out once I started using them in my hiring process. For every 10 packets I sent out, I usually received five of them back. Of those five, perhaps only one or two would be someone I wanted to hire. This may not seem like a good response rate but believe me, it was great! Identifying one or two potentially perfect candidates without having to personally interview a large number of applicants who would turn out to be unsuitable is precisely how the application packet saved me many, many hours of effort. And when you utilize an application packet as a part of your hiring process, it will save you that effort, too. I promise!

Finally, if you get more quality packets back than you need, make a "Future Pet Sitters or Dog Walkers" file for any applications you can't use right away. When you notify the qualified applicant that you are hiring someone else, you can let them know you're saving their application for later. That way, when you are ready to hire more people or are in a pinch and need someone right away, you can refer back to that file. Obviously not every applicant who applied months or even a year before will still be available or interested in the job, but it will be a great place to start when you have an emergency or if a staff member quits suddenly.

Why an Application Packet Works

You might be asking yourself why you have to bother with a full application packet instead of just a simple one-page job application or applicant resumes. The application packet may seem like such a simple, low-tech hiring tool, but it *works*. It worked for me in my own business and it has worked for thousands of my coaching clients around the world.

The application packet is so successful precisely because it requires more than merely submitting a resume. It necessitates time, work, and commitment. The applicants who are willing to fill it out and send it back to you show dedication right from the very beginning. It doesn't mean they are absolutely going to be the right match for your company, but it substantially increases the odds that they will!

Before I started using the application packet, my dog walkers and pet sitters would stay with my company for around four to six months. After I started having candidates fill out the application packet and changed how I scheduled staff members (I explain more about scheduling and avoiding staff burnout in Chapters 11 and 12), the average jumped to three to five years and beyond. It showed me who was committed and really wanted this job long term.

When you hire in your own pet sitting and dog walking business, you want committed applicants that are professional and pay close attention to detail. You will be able to see which applicants have these characteristics simply by reviewing their packets. Pay close attention to their responses and you will know a lot about

YOU WILL GET A HIGHER CALIBER OF APPLICANTS AS A RESULT OF INTEGRATING AN APPLICATION PACKET INTO YOUR HIRING SYSTEM. I GUARANTEE IT.

them before you ever meet. You will get a higher caliber of applicants as a result of integrating an application packet into your hiring system. I guarantee it.

Kristin's Story:

Using an application packet completely revolutionized my hiring experience. Before I created the application packet, I absolutely dreaded hiring someone new. Everything about the hiring process was so exhausting.

Before the application packet was "born," I spent so much time on the phone and conducting face-to-face interviews with potential applicants. Most of the applicants were such terrible fits for my business that I would feel overwhelmed and discouraged because of how much time I wasted trying to hire without actually finding anyone I wanted to work for me. Instead of making my job easier (which was the reason I wanted to hire help in the first place), I was totally stressed and behind on my work.

After I had my epiphany, created my "hiring assistant," and started utilizing the application packet I'd created, I'd find out so much about each applicant before I'd even talked on the phone with them! I would go through the packets at my leisure and set up interviews to meet with the most promising candidates, drastically reducing the amount of time I spent on phone calls and in-person interviews.

Hiring Success Stories:

"I had been a solo pet sitter for 11 years because I could not bring myself to trust someone else with my hard-earned reputation. I was quickly approaching burnout. In desperation, I decided to try Kristin's Pet Sitting and Dog Walking Hiring Kit, which contains the Application Packet and many other hiring items. Kristin had said, 'You will get the best of the best working with you if you follow my hiring system'. Sounds like an 'as seen on TV' pitch, right?!

Thank God it wasn't. Honestly, I would have never hired the person I did without following the set of guidelines that Kristin gives in the hiring kit. The woman I ended up hiring had a lot of tattoos, dressed differently than I would expect, and was not exactly what I had in mind. I held my breath and we signed on the dotted line and I was thinking, 'Surely Kristin wouldn't sell us this hiring kit if it didn't work'.

In the end, the 'strange' girl with piercings, tattoos and unusual clothes was perfect for my business. She ran my entire operation while I went to Europe for three weeks and did an excellent job."
Gina Triay - Tall Tails Pet Sitting, LLC
Slidell, Louisiana

"*After the supportive, honest, and professional coaching from Kristin, and due to my desire to actually manage my business instead of 'doing' the business, I decided to purchase the Application Packet and the Welcome Packet for the New Staff Member. What at first seemed overwhelming in terms of screening and hiring complete strangers for my business became a fun, enjoyable, and completely streamlined event once I had the Application Packet for Staff Members to use and follow as my guide.*

The best thing about the Application Packet for Staff Members is that you get a completely clear picture of interested applications before you even meet with the applicants! The review of the Application Packets has now become one of the activities I look forward to most as a business owner."
Brandon Burton - Big Sky Dogs
Pasadena, California

Action Step

Using the sample emails included in the "How to Use Your Application Packet" section of the chapter, compose two email drafts you will be able to use to respond to potential job applicants: one for applicants that are not a good fit, and one to accompany your application packet. If the emails work for you exactly as they are written already, simply insert your business information and you'll be all set. Having these emails composed before you post the job listing will save you a lot of time when you start getting responses.

Action Step

Create an application packet for potential candidates. Be sure to include each of the items under the "Creating Your Own Application Packet" heading.

Again, if you don't have the time or desire to make your own packet, or if you'd like to read what I include in the packet I developed for myself and other pet sitters and dog walkers, you can purchase my customizable Application Packet here and edit it as little or as much as you need to for your own business needs: www.SFPSA.com/packet.

Action Step

Review your application packet to make sure it does not include any intentional or accidental discriminatory questions. You cannot legally ask for any information that "might be reasonably understood as indicating an intention to discriminate" based on gender, race, religion, national origin, age, or disability. Run your application by an employment lawyer if you have any questions about whether or not it meets state and federal guidelines as listed at www.eeoc.gov.

Action Step

In your hiring success journal, make a list of five to seven open-ended questions to ask potential candidates in your application packet. These should be questions that give you a good idea of how each candidate will handle situations that arise in your business. If you're having trouble coming up with ideas, think about challenging situations that have occurred for you or other staff you've hired. When you finish the list, choose your favorite three questions to include in your application packet.

EIGHT

Find Exceptional Pet Sitters and Dog Walkers

Where and How to Place Help Wanted Ads That Get Results

"Hiring the right people takes time, good questions, and a healthy dose of curiosity."

–Richard Branson

Once you've released your fear of letting go and realized the advantages that hiring will give you professionally and personally, it's time to actually find the very best pet sitters and dog walkers to share the day-to-day work of your business.

So many of the problems business owners have with those they hire can be avoided by hiring the right people in the first place. This chapter will go over what you need to know about advertising your open positions in order to attract quality candidates every time.

Be Clear from the Beginning

The most helpful technique for finding a "perfect fit" staff member is to be exceptionally clear what you are looking for from the very beginning.

By clearly stating the expected hours, responsibilities, and pay, you'll quickly weed out unsuitable candidates. Ask applicants to fill out the application packet (as opposed to simply submitting a resume) to help you narrow down the applicant pool. You may limit the number of applicants slightly by listing specifics in your help wanted ad, but you will be sure to attract a higher percentage of those who are legitimately interested in the job.

What details should you include in your help wanted ad? Put yourself in the position of a job applicant and ask yourself what you would want to know.

At the very least, include the following basics in your job posting:

- **A clear title/first line:** You want to catch the eye of potential applicants right away. People often read the title and/or the first line of a posting and then move on, so be sure to say what you mean from the very beginning. Instead of, "The primary duties of this position are ..." start with something like this, "Reliable and caring pet sitter in Bakersfield needed."

- **Required duties:** Are you hiring a mid-day dog walker? A pet sitter who can do pet visits? Someone who can do both? State what you need in the ad, as well as whether or not prior experience (and how much) is preferred or required. If you are looking for someone with special training or certification, be sure to say so — but only if you will truly only accept certified candidates. You do not want to discourage otherwise ideal applicants that only lack training that is simple for you to provide after they are working for you.

- **The geographical area(s) where you need staff coverage:** There is no point in interviewing candidates that live a long distance from the service area you are hiring for. Even if they are willing to make the long drive to work, they will not stay. Reducing staff drive times to 10-15 minutes each way is crucial for retention. People may say they are willing to make a long commute, but most of the time, that willingness drops off quickly once they experience a few weeks or months of traffic to and from work. Although it is not legal in many states to refuse to interview or hire someone based on where they live, you will save yourself some of the hassle and headache of replacing dog walkers and pet sitters if you clearly state where the work will take place so applicants will know from the very beginning how far they'd need to travel to get to work.

- **The days of the week and times of day needed:** If you know when you need additional help with dog walks and pet visits (and you should be clear on this if you completed all of the *Action Steps* at the end of the last chapter), include that information in your ad. You want to attract applicants that are available to work when you need them. Save everyone involved (including yourself!) time and effort by clearly stating the available hours in the help wanted ad.

- **Brief details about the expected pay:** While specifics of pay rates and schedules can wait until the interview, it is a good idea to include basic details in your posting. If you are only hiring for a part-time position, you want applicants to know this is supplemental income, for example, and not a full-time position. If you already know how much you plan to pay new staff members, include that in the listing. Advertising your pay rate can also be a good way to attract high-quality dog walkers and pet sitters if you are willing to pay more than your competitors. If you haven't settled on a final rate, go back to Chapter 6 for details on how much to pay.

In situations where you are limited to a certain number of lines or words for each posting, you may have to further narrow down this list. In such cases, start with what is most important and continue until you run out of room/lines/words. Remember that you want to strike just the right balance so you attract as many of the best candidates as possible while still weeding out those that are unqualified or unsuitable for your job.

Where to Advertise

Imagine your ideal applicant. Where would you expect this person to find your help wanted ad? Knowing what you are looking for will help you narrow down your choices.

Here are some of the most successful places business owners have advertised and found high-quality applicants:

- **Craigslist:** Craigslist is one of the largest online job boards in the world and gives you the chance to find lots of candidates with just one posting. In some cities, you will need to pay a fee to post in the "Jobs" section, whereas it is generally free to list your job under "Gigs." Even if you live in a free area, I do recommend paying to post your ad in "Jobs" under "Etc./Misc." because you will get so much more exposure that way. You may need to be patient with your Craigslist ad as responses sometimes come in waves. There may be some weeks, months, or seasons where you only get a slow trickle of responses and other time periods where you have a flood of qualified candidates. Be willing to experiment and, if after a few tries, you find that Craigslist isn't working for you, simply move on to the other options on this list.

- **Facebook Jobs:** I know quite a few pet business owners that have had success finding high-quality applicants through Facebook Jobs. You can create a job post right on Facebook by navigating to the Facebook Jobs page that will show up on your business Facebook page and on the Facebook Jobs bookmark. Although the basic listing is free, I do recommend paying to boost your ad to reach a much wider pool of candidates. With the boost feature, you can specify the target audience, which can help you find job seekers who have skills and interests that match your business.

- **Indeed.com:** Indeed is a traditional job site where you post an ad and browse potential applicants' resumes. Many pet sitting and dog walking business owners have had a lot of hiring success from using this site.

- **Nextdoor.com:** Nextdoor is a location-based social media site that enables residents and business owners in a particular area to form localized social networks. The great advantage to advertising on Nextdoor is that it is very localized and will help you connect with applicants near your target location.

- **Care.com:** Care.com is a website where caregivers (including those offering pet care) can advertise their services. I have some coaching clients who have had great success contacting people already offering dog walking and pet sitting on the Care.com site and asking if they'd like to apply for a position in addition to the work they are doing on their own.

- **Pet Stores, Pet Grooming Shops, and Veterinarians' Offices:** Many of the best candidates for pet sitting and dog walking jobs are pet owners themselves. By advertising in places that pet owners shop and visit, you will have a better chance of finding applicants who are good with pets. Some vet offices will not allow you to post your ad if they consider it a conflict of interest (offices that offer boarding or similar pet care services, for example). Even still, it's worth approaching local vet offices and asking if you can post on their bulletin board. Not every vet's office will say yes, but the ones that do can be a great way to find quality candidates.

- **Mothers' Clubs:** Stay-at-home parents can be a great hiring resource because they often have regular schedules and are often already involved in the community. If you want to reach the stay-at-home parents in your area, advertise in mothers' club newsletters. Do an internet search for mothers' club newsletters in your town to find options in your area. Many mothers' clubs have online newsletters, while some still snail mail physical newsletters to their members.

- **College Job Boards:** College students are often available during the day a few days a week and looking for extra income. I especially like that many students have summers and holidays off from school, which lines up perfectly with the busiest times of year for most pet sitters.

- **Local Newsletters and Bulletin Boards:** Since you are looking for applicants that love animals, focus first on bulletin boards or newsletters that cater to animal owners, such as the local shelter bulletin board or humane society newsletter. Hang flyers or index cards with tear-off tabs that say, "Dog walker and pet sitter wanted". Putting pet images on the advertisements will draw the eye and get attention. Coffee shops, churches, and libraries often have job and notice boards as well. Also, some churches will allow you to pay a small amount to post your job listing in their church bulletin.

Remember to focus on posting your advertisement in the geo-graphical area where the work will take place. Doing so will increase the chances that you will find candidates that live within a reasonable driving distance.

Find Help in Unexpected Places

You may also find, as many business owners do, high-quality applicants in nontraditional ways. Whether that means putting a "help wanted" notice on your vehicle when you travel for dog walks and pet visits or through referrals from current clients and staff members.

The first step to getting referrals of people who would be great for your business is to get the word out that you are hiring:

- **If you already have staff members working for you, ask them to recommend anyone they know that would be a good fit.** You will get even more quality recommendations from them if you offer a substantial referral bonus for any hire they recommended that ends up working for the business for at least three months.

- **Send an email to your friends and family along with a link to your current job posting.** Hiring people you know personally can sometimes backfire, so be very selective if you decide to go that route, but taking referrals from people you trust often leads to quality candidates you might not have found otherwise.

- **Your current clients can also be a source of hiring referrals.** That said, I would be very careful about any email or communication with clients about hiring referrals so that they don't panic when they see you are hiring. If you do ask clients for hiring recommendations, make sure to specify that you are looking for responsible, dependable, and professional pet lovers so your clients feel assured that you are only going to hire the very best staff.

- **Some business owners have ended up hiring their own clients with great success.** Occasionally, you may have a client ask if you are hiring. If you enjoy working with them as a client, they may end up being a great staff member as well. If you think they would be a good fit, direct them to the job posting or simply give them an application packet. Still, proceed with caution. If they turn out not to be a good hire, you will likely lose them as a client as well.

Avoid Discrimination

You may have a perfect candidate in your mind, but specifically stating that you are looking for a college student, stay-at-home mom, or candidate of a certain age is a form of discrimination. You must be careful to avoid discriminatory hiring for two reasons. First, you may be missing out on the perfect applicant without even realizing it. Second, it is against federal law to discriminate against job applicants because of their race, color, religion, gender/sex, national origin, age, or disability. Many states have additional protections, including prohibiting geographical discrimination.

There are certain things you cannot say in your job posting in order to avoid illegal discrimination. Terms like "hard-working" and "flexible schedule" are allowed, whereas "young college student with lots of energy" is not. If you prefer staff members that are bilingual in another language, you can include that in your ad as long as there is a work-related justification. As long as you're not excluding anyone based on race or ethnicity, you can list qualifications that you'd like applicants to have. "Spanish speaking is a plus" would be acceptable, while "Hispanic applicants preferred" would not. By saying that being bilingual is preferred, you are further protected because no one can argue that you are excluding people who don't speak Spanish.

In the case of a dispute, criteria that can be shown to have a discriminatory intent are illegal. If you have any question about whether or not your job posting meets legal requirements, visit the Equal Employment Opportunity Commission's website for employers at www.eeoc.gov or talk to an employment lawyer in your area. It's always better to check beforehand than to deal with a discrimination lawsuit down the road.

Make Your "Help Wanted" Ad Stand Out

This is your chance to highlight the key values of your business. Applicants will want to get a feel for what the company culture is like as well as what their day-to-day duties will be. The way that you write your ad will go a long way to projecting what matters to you, whether it's trustworthiness, cheerfulness, or professionalism. Make your ad friendly, upbeat, and reflective of your business values.

If you have a mission statement or statement of purpose for your business, incorporate some of the same language into your job posting. If not, think about what sets your company apart from the competition. Is it how much you care about your clients? Are you always on time and careful to leave clients' homes clean and orderly? Do you offer more reliable hours to your staff? Highlight whatever makes your company unique and attractive in your job posting. Yes, you are looking for the best candidates, but the best candidates are also looking for a company that they can believe in.

> YES, YOU ARE LOOKING FOR THE BEST CANDIDATES, BUT THE BEST CANDIDATES ARE ALSO LOOKING FOR A COMPANY THAT THEY CAN BELIEVE IN.

Here are two sample help wanted ads that you can use or modify for your own business.

For mid-day dog walks:

Mid-Day Dog Walkers Needed: M/W/F or T/TH

[Your Business Here] is an established and well-loved pet sitting and dog walking company, and we are seeking exceptional dog walkers to add to our great staff.

Days: M/W/F or T/TH
Hours: 10-1 or 11-2

Pay rate: $ [Insert your rate]/per dog, per 45-minute walk.
Walkers needed in: [Insert your cities/areas]

Please note: This is a very part-time job to start (2-5 walks per week). More walks available as business increases. Walks are for 1-2 dogs at a time; more dogs possible as business and your skill increase.

Requirements:
- You have a car (a dog-friendly car if you want to walk multiple dogs from different homes).
- You LOVE dogs.
- You feel comfortable walking both BIG and small dogs.
- You can work with us until at least [Insert date that is 6-12 months away]. The pets will want to develop a long-term relationship with you.
- You are available for the days/hours listed above.
- You can easily pass a criminal/background check.

Please e-mail us at [Insert your e-mail address], and in 50 words or less, explain why you would be the perfect person for this job. Also, please include the days/hours you are available and your location. Thanks!

For daytime pet visits:

AM/PM Pet Visitors Needed

[Your Business Here] is an established and well-loved pet sitting company, and we are seeking exceptional pet visitors to add to our staff.

Please note: We will be accepting applications until we find the right staff, so if you are viewing this posting weeks after it's been published, please contact us as we may still need more staff members!

Pet visitors needed in: [Insert areas needed]

Information regarding visits:
- One-two visits per day for 3-14 days. (You'll provide feeding, walking, plant watering, and mail pickup while clients are traveling.)
- Visits for dogs are 30 to 45 minutes between 7-9 am and 6-8 pm. (Perfect for someone who wants to supplement his/her income before and after a full-time job.)
- Visit times for cats are more flexible and are usually once daily for 30-minutes.

Requirements for the dog and cat visitor position:
- You have a car.
- You can commit to working with us until at least [Insert date that is 6-12 months away].
- You love both dogs and cats.
- You are available for both morning and evening visits.
- You can work at least two of the three major winter holidays:
  Thanksgiving, Christmas, New Year's (Don't worry; you'll be able to have a holiday too, and you'll also be paid more per visit during this time).
- You can pass a criminal/background check.

Hours/Pay rate: [Insert the approximate number of visits needed each week as well as the range of hours/pay per visit.]

Please e-mail us at [Insert your e-mail address], and in 50 words or less, explain why you would be the perfect person for this job. Thanks!

Feel free to modify these help wanted ads or use them as inspiration as you write your own. Please note, for example, that in some states it is illegal to discriminate against applicants with a criminal record. As always, check with an employment lawyer familiar with your area for clarification on the law in your state. If you would like an electronic template of these two ads as well as an overnight pet sitter advertisement, you can purchase all three as part of my hiring kit at www.SFPSA.com/hire.

Kristin's Story:

Early on in my business, I had a neighbor who asked if she could work for me while she was between jobs. We were close friends as well as neighbors, so I assumed she'd be a great staff member. Not the case! What we quickly found is that we both had a hard time with the shift in our relationship once I was her boss. After a couple of weeks, we both realized that her working for me was not a good fit for either of us and we parted our working relationship amicably and resumed our friendship (whew!).

On the other hand, I've also had positive experiences hiring people I know. I once had a client of many years call me out of the blue one day and ask if she could work for me. She said she loved animals and really wanted to spend her time taking care of them. I was hesitant because she was a client, but she was available and willing right when I needed to hire someone, so I decided to take a leap and hire her. She ended up being one of the best pet sitters and dog walkers I had and stayed with my company for 8 years!

Because I've had both good and bad experiences when hiring people I know, I've learned to be very thoughtful about who I hire, especially when they are a part of my life already.

Hiring Success Stories:

"One of my clients called me and asked if I needed help, so I gave her a chance. She has been doing an awesome job, and she came to me!"
Tracy Lewallen - Posh Pooches Pet Sitting
Simpsonville, South Carolina

"I got one of those car window markers and wrote on my back window 'Now Hiring Pet Sitters'. I stopped at a cafe for lunch one day and the girl behind the counter asked me about it. She has been one of my best pet sitters for the past 17 months!"
Sherry Nichols - Creature Comforts Pet Sitting Service
Sierra Vista, Arizona

Action Step

If you haven't already finished creating your application packet (or if you haven't yet purchased one from the website: www.SFPSA. com/packet), be sure to do that before placing your help wanted ad so you'll be ready to respond as soon as possible when candidates start contacting you.

Action Step

Spend 10 minutes browsing help wanted ads online to see what other pet sitting and dog walking companies in your area are looking for. If you see any help wanted ads for pet care businesses as you visit pet stores and veterinarians' offices, read those as well. When an ad stands out to you, make a note in your hiring success journal, detailing exactly what about that ad appeals to you.

Action Step

Write a sample job advertisement of your own, using the bullet points at the beginning of this chapter and the example help wanted ads as a template. Have a friend look at the ad and give you feedback. Ask your friend if the ad clearly conveys what kind of applicant you are looking for.

Action Step

Read through your help wanted ad for clarity and any potential discriminatory language. Check the Equal Employment Opportunity Commission's website for employers at www.eeoc.gov under the Employer/Small Business tab to see what is considered illegal discrimination and/or have an employment lawyer look over the ad.

Action Step

Using the ideas in the "Where to Advertise" section, make a list of places to post your advertisement after you have your application packet and hiring paperwork ready. If you plan to post it on bulletin or job boards in your area, make a list in your hiring success journal of the locations and any specific details you will need. Some places limit the size of anything placed on the board, for example. Aim for at least five physical postings in addition to one online listing. If you have an urgent need to find someone, start with three online listings instead.

NINE

Interview With Confidence

Choose the Best Candidates for Your Pet Business

"I'd rather interview 50 people and not hire anyone than hire the wrong person."

–Jeff Bezos

So many future employee problems can be avoided by establishing clear expectations at the very beginning. I will go over interview tips and questions that you can use to conduct focused interviews so you and your job applicants will leave the interview with more information than you both had going in. Whether this will be your first time conducting interviews or you have plenty of experience interviewing job applicants, this chapter will help you hone your interview skills and be able to confidently decide who to hire and who not to hire for your business.

Before the Interview

Just a short amount of preparation will make all the difference when you sit down to interview candidates.

Here are some important steps you can take before you start each in-person interview:

1. **Tell candidates what to expect beforehand.** You really want to get a clear picture of how each candidate will fit in your company during the interview, but that won't happen if the job

applicants are too nervous to be themselves. Consider giving each applicant a brief idea of what to expect in the interview so they can relax and give you a clearer picture of what they are really like. Confirming the interview time and place and telling them the types of questions you may ask are ways you can help candidates feel more at ease ... and more able to represent themselves accurately.

2. **Review the job posting.** Take a few minutes to look over the applicable job posting before each interview. Doing so will help you remember job specifics, such as the job duties and days/times you need staffed. You will probably find this especially helpful if you are hiring for more than one position or time slot at the same time.

3. **Look through the completed application packet again.** You'll want to make the most of your time with each candidate. Looking through the application packet again on the day of the interview will help you avoid asking questions you already have answers to and give you a chance to determine specific questions you'd like to ask. Make notes to use during the interview.

4. **Get there early.** Make sure you are at the interview location well before the set time so you can mentally prepare yourself and scope out the best spot available. Getting there early will also help you evaluate whether the applicant arrived on time. Timeliness is an important trait for them to have, given that they'll be meeting clients for meet-and-greets and agreeing to be at pet care jobs on time (every time) if they're hired.

Where to Have the Interview

When it comes to choosing where to hold your interviews, choose a public place (for everyone's safety) and preferably one that is pet friendly. I recommend outdoor coffee shops that allow dogs. Dog parks or even the picnic table at a regular park are suitable options as well.

I suggest that pet-friendly locations be at the top of your list of interview location choices so that you can take a dog along and see how the applicants interact with pets as part of the interview. You can have them walk the dog and observe how they interact and how comfortable they are. A large and slightly unruly dog, but not so unruly that you can't focus on the interview, can give you a great idea of how each applicant will handle a similar dog during a walk or visit since not all potential clients' dogs will be well behaved. Look for candidates who are also comfortable interacting with people and who genuinely seem to love animals.

If you can't bring a dog with you, definitely aim to have the interview at or near a dog park so you can observe how each applicant interacts with the dogs at the park. If you're at a coffee shop, make sure that you can sit outside so that you're able to watch your potential staff member interact with the dog freely.

The Best Questions to Ask

Before you conduct your first interview, it's a great idea to have a standard list of four to five interview questions ready to go. You won't need to ask as many questions as you might think because you'll have gained so much information earlier from reviewing the application packet. Once you've gone through each application packet while preparing for the interviews, you should know a lot about the candidates before you've even met them in person.

If you've never conducted an interview or are looking to refine your skill, you might have turned to this chapter hoping to find specific questions.

With that in mind, I've included three types of questions and a few examples of each:

- **Open-ended questions.** Many business owners ask a lot of yes or no questions, which I suggest you avoid. Most candidates are going to try to give you the answers they think you want to hear. What you really want is to ask questions that get them talking honestly instead of just giving rote responses. Open-ended questions will give you a much more complete picture of each applicant and their skill level.

Example questions: Tell me about your own pets. Have you ever had to deal with any pet medical emergencies? What kind of pets do you enjoy caring for the most?

- **Questions that clear up any concerns you have.** The interview is your chance to get specifics about your candidates' experience, work history, and/or expectations for the job. If there is anything in the application that you'd like to know more about, bring it up during the interview.

Example questions: How have your previous jobs and pet experiences prepared you for this position? What is the best method for pilling a cat?

- **Specific "what would you do" questions about pet care.** I like to ask questions about how they would respond to situations I've personally experienced while caring for pets myself or heard about from my pet sitters and dog walkers. This type of question gives you the chance to evaluate applicants' understanding of pet care and also how they might handle an emergency.

Example questions: What would you do if you came into the house and the pet is unusually lethargic? How would you handle it if you showed up at a cat sitting job and couldn't find the cat?

Since you are going to limit each interview to around five questions or fewer, be selective about which questions give you the best idea of how well a candidate will fit in your business.

Trusting Your Intuition/Gut Instinct

In the end, the most important characteristics of the best hires is that they be (1) someone you want to work with and (2) someone your clients will feel confident trusting with their homes and pets. For most business owners, that means someone you can trust, who follows through with what they've been hired to do and is pleasant to be around. Based on your personal and professional experiences up to this point, you may have other traits that are important to you as well.

I tend to examine the application packet thoroughly, and after the face-to-face interview, I go with my intuition when it comes to hiring. I trust how I feel both when I'm reviewing information gained from the packet and when I have the potential applicant in front of me. If they both feel like a strong YES, I tend to hire them. I suggest you do the same, as well as getting a background check on the potential hire after the face-to-face meeting (more on how and where to get background checks in the next chapter). After all, every hire that you make ultimately reflects on you as the business owner. You absolutely want to be comfortable with each person you invite into your work "family", and you want your clients to feel comfortable with the people you've hired, too.

You may need to cultivate your gut instinct, or it may come naturally to you already. Most of us, especially those of us who work with animals, have that innate ability to "read" people. Animals are very intuitive, and if we're around them a lot, we often are as well, simply through osmosis. So, listen to your gut instinct. I've found that the more I trust that voice inside (my gut/intuition), the louder it will get until it becomes a heightened sense of awareness. This has served me well in hiring and it will serve you well, too, if you cultivate and heed that inner knowing.

I can't tell you the number of coaching clients I've worked with who have had a challenging staff member and will freely admit, "There were red flags during the interview, but I overlooked them, thinking they would change, or they didn't matter very much".

> I'VE FOUND THAT THE MORE I TRUST THAT VOICE INSIDE (MY GUT/INTUITION), THE LOUDER IT WILL GET UNTIL IT BECOMES A HEIGHTENED SENSE OF AWARENESS.

In addition to listening to your intuition, you also want to pay attention to more tangible, outward signs you may notice that an applicant won't be the right fit for your company. These signs can show up in the application packet or in the interview itself. For example, non-verbal communication during the interview is as important as what a candidate says and will tell you a lot about the applicant as a person.

I once had an experience that really shows why paying attention to these non-verbal cues matters. I had a dog with me at an interview (like I often did) and he pawed at the applicant once or twice and rubbed against her legs to try and get her attention. She did not pet him or even look at him at all while he was pawing her. In fact, she started picking fur off of her clothes and putting it on the ground during the interview. I just couldn't imagine how she would fit into my company if she went to client interviews and didn't even pet the dogs and then picked fur off her clothes in front of the client. Though she seemed to enjoy talking to me, I could see she wasn't enthusiastic about working with animals and, thus, wouldn't be a good fit for my company.

Another detail to notice is the impression you get when you first meet each applicant. The applicants don't have to be dressed up or look a certain way (nor should they), but you do want someone that will put your clients at ease. Do they present themselves well? Do they look you in the eye when they talk? That's really important. Clients are going to feel uncomfortable if your staff member isn't able to hold eye contact.

Do they seem confident and comfortable with you, but not cocky? I had a couple of people I interviewed in the course of my business who I would describe as cocky or arrogant, and that is a very different energy than confidence. I made the mistake years ago of hiring some-body who was so conceited that it was a challenge to work together. Again, follow your intuition on this. Pick the people that make you feel like they'll treat everyone well: your clients (human and pet), you, and your other staff.

The final thing that you want to ask yourself is whether this is someone that you'd feel comfortable with in *your* home. If you find it hard to answer that question, try asking it about your loved ones: Would you feel comfortable having this person help your mom or close friend who might need a pet sitter or dog walker? Would you want the person you are interviewing taking care of a beloved family member or friend's home and pets? Again, trust your intuition and your impression of the applicant during the face-to-face meeting.

After the Interview

If you can tell right away that the person you are interviewing will not work for the position, keep the interview short. You don't want to waste their time (or your own). You can tell the applicant that you will be doing a short interview today and then a longer, second interview with the final candidates. That way, they know that you will follow up and either schedule another interview or notify them that you've hired someone else. After you've finished all your interviews, you can send them an email and tell them you've made another hire. Thank them for their time spent filling out the application packet and let them know that you'll be shredding their application packet to keep their personal information confidential.

And what should you do after an interview goes well? I suggest you wait until you've finished all your interviews before making a final decision. Then, select the applicant(s) you think will be the best fit for your company and extend a job offer to them on the phone or via email. I'll go over how to get your staff member started off on the right foot in the next chapter.

Kristin's Story:

In my early days of hiring, I conducted a lot of interviews in one single day, often back to back. Because of this, I would sometimes get confused about which applicant I thought would be the best after a long round of conducting interviews. I eventually developed a system to help me remember how I felt about each candidate at the end of the day.

After the applicant left and before the next interviewee arrived, I wrote a number between 1-10 at the top of the application packet. (The number one indicated an absolute "no" as far as hiring and the number 10 was an absolute "yes".) I also made notes below the number — whatever impressions stood out to me the most about this person (good and bad): "Seems like a kind and responsible person; didn't look me in the eyes for most of the interview, which made feel like I couldn't trust her; he's experienced with difficult dogs; she prefers cats over dogs, etc."

At the end of all the interviews, I would review the packets and pay special attention to my notes and the number I gave each one. If I wasn't clear who was the right hire immediately after each interview, reviewing my notes and the number at the top of each packet nearly always gave me the clarity I needed.

Hiring Success Stories:

"A question I like to ask potential pet sitters and dog walkers is: 'What dog breed do you most identify with?' Asking this question helps me find out how they see themselves, as well as a little about their breed knowledge!"
Marcy Santos - The Right Fluff Pet Sitting
Rockville, Maryland

"When I'm doing a face-to-face interview with an applicant, I like asking this question: 'Tell me about a time you decided to take an animal to the vet (either your own or a friend's pet). What signs brought you to that decision?'"
Heather May Izatt - Puget Paws, LLC
Shoreline, Washington

Action Step

Get ready for your interviews by reading through the application packets of every candidate you will interview. I suggest doing this the night before or early in the morning of the interview so the information will be fresh in your mind when you meet with them. Highlight parts of the packet that you have questions about or that you want to make sure to ask the applicant. Then, make notes on the packet so you have talking points ready to go at the interview.

Action Step

Find one or two good interview locations near your home. Look for a relaxed atmosphere where you can bring a dog. On the day of the interview, plan to arrive early to find the most comfortable place so you can sit and talk to your potential new hire without interruption.

Action Step

Using the guidelines and sample questions in the "What Questions to Ask" section of this chapter, write a list of interview questions. Aim for four or five open-ended questions that you can ask each candidate. Write these questions in your hiring success journal so you have them to refer back to during your interviews.

Action Step

Trusting your intuition is an incredibly important part of the interview process. Here is an exercise to practice listening to your gut: Start with a brief period of quiet stillness, sitting comfortably where you will not be interrupted and where you are free from distractions. Make sure your hiring success journal is nearby so you can reach it without leaving your quiet spot at the end of the exercise. Set your timer for five minutes. Before you begin, ask yourself a question that you'd like clarity on. If you don't have a specific question in mind, you can simply spend that time listening to your surroundings and simply noticing how you feel. At the end of the five minutes, set your timer for an additional five minutes and record any thoughts or ideas you had during your period of calm in your hiring success journal. Often getting quiet and still can help create clarity. Even a short five-minute period of silent stillness can reveal a lot!

Action Step

Once you extend a job offer to an applicant, reward yourself. Hiring is a big step in any business! If you've followed the *Action Steps* in the book to this point, you have put in diligent work to make sure you are hiring in the best way for your business ... and that can be exhausting. Self-care is so important, especially for business owners. Today or this week, celebrate making the hire by treating yourself to an item or activity that is nourishing to you.

TEN

Get New Staff Members Started Off Right

Train Your Employees and Introduce Them to Your Clients

"The only thing worse than training your employees and having them leave is not training them and having them stay."

–Henry Ford

Congratulations! You have taken a huge step and hired the staff member(s) you've been looking for. After all the time you've spent getting to this point, you deserve a big pat on the back (and that tangible reward for yourself that was part of the *Action Steps* in the last chapter!). But the work isn't done yet. Now you need to get each new staff member fitting within your business and working with your existing clients.

Background Checks and Welcome Packet

Whether or not you run background checks on new staff members is a personal decision, but I do recommend it. Since the pet sitting and dog walking business involves access to people's homes and beloved pets, routine background checks on all applicants you plan to hire can help give you and your clients peace of mind.

Members of some pet sitting organizations can order discounted background checks or you can just do an internet search for "low-cost background checks" for current prices.

I also recommend you create a "welcome packet" to give every new staff member. I developed my own welcome packet early on in my hiring process when I had new pet sitters come back and ask me, "What exactly am I supposed to do at each pet visit or dog walk?"

You can create your own welcome packet or purchase the fully customizable Welcome Packet for the New Staff Member available on my website and edit for your own business: www.SFPSA.com/welcome.

If you decide to create your own welcome packet, it should include all the information they need to begin work:

- **A policy and procedure list.** A written description of company expectations and procedures will give staff members something to refer to before they come to you with questions.

- **Client interview sheet.** Staff members will use these during client interviews so they can ask all the right questions to obtain the information your business needs from each client.

- **Checklists for each type of job.** These checklists will detail everything you expect to be done at each dog walk, pet visit, or overnight pet sit. This is especially helpful for staff members who have limited experience with professional dog walking and pet sitting.

- **An employee contract.** I suggest including a very detailed contract about what will and will not be included in your new staff member's job. It's a good idea to include a non-compete clause to prevent staff members from taking your clients with them if they leave to start their own pet care business.

Even if you do include a non-compete clause in your contract, you should be aware that it's very expensive to actually pursue damages if a staff member takes your clients. I had that happen with two of my staff members, and it was really painful for me. I could have enforced the non-compete clause, but it would have been so expensive that I just let it go. So, unless you want to spend a lot of money fighting a legal battle, all you can really do is have them sign a non-compete clause so that they are aware that they're not supposed to take your clients if/when they leave your company. But again, they might still do it. However, since most people who are working for you don't want to be their own boss, don't let this keep you from making a hire. Although it does happen, in my experience, it is relatively rare.

Remember, if you are using independent contractors, many of these items in the welcome packet are not allowed or must be modified. You cannot give specifics about how a job is completed to an independent contractor, for example. You will need to create an IC-friendly welcome packet if you plan to hire independent contractors instead of employees. Like I outlined in the Employee vs. Independent Contractor chapter, misclassifying staff members can be an expensive mistake. Be sure to run your welcome packet documents by an employment lawyer if you are hiring independent contractors to make sure each document is within the legal requirements.

> YOU WILL NEED TO CREATE AN IC-FRIENDLY WELCOME PACKET IF YOU PLAN TO HIRE INDEPENDENT CONTRACTORS INSTEAD OF EMPLOYEES.

The Employee Handbook

In addition to a welcome packet, I suggest you create an employee handbook to give to each new employee. This will provide even more detailed information for your new hires and save you from having to answer the same basic questions over and over again. Remember, one of the reasons you decided to hire in the first place was to create more time in your day, not to fill it up with even more busy work (like answering a lot of questions from staff). The right employee handbook will help you cover all the bases with staff and will clearly detail what should and should not be done during their employment.

If, instead of creating your own from scratch, you would prefer to purchase a ready-made employee handbook that is fully editable so you can customize it for your business, you will find a 54-page Employee Handbook at www.SFPSA.com/employee.

Whether you purchase the Employee Handbook from the site or create your own from scratch, your employee handbook should include the following:

- **Legal documentation.** Your employment lawyer can walk you through what you are legally obligated to provide and the items that should go in your employee handbook. Examples include employee classification, at-will notice, and equal employment compliance. Again, some of these are required under federal law and some are state specific, so definitely consult with a local attorney.

- **Conduct and behavior expectations.** Protect your business by outlining, in writing, what behaviors are expected (and those that are prohibited) *before* the first day of work.

- **Details on compensation.** You will want to clearly outline the pay rate, pay periods, any bonuses, and overtime policies.

- **Benefits and leave.** Depending on your state, you will need to provide information on leave for holidays, jury duty, military service, medical care, family obligations, and voting.

- **Health, safety, and security.** This is where you will outline your drug and alcohol policies, as well as information on workplace safety and workers' compensation.

- **Workplace guidelines.** Specific information about attendance and tardiness, dress code and personal appearance, cell phone use, photography in clients' homes, and conflicts of interest all fall under this category.

- **Employment separation.** Avoid problems from the very start by clearly defining what happens if they get fired, what employees should do if they need to resign, and what is expected of each employee at the end of their employment.

So much of what goes into your employee handbook will protect you as the business owner and your business reputation. If you have ever been afraid that hiring would reduce the quality of your service, hiring the right people and giving them the most complete information possible in an employee handbook will go a long way in alleviating that fear. Give each new hire a date by which they need to finish their review of the handbook. Have them read the handbook closely and sign that they have read and understand everything included inside.

> **Hiring Tip:**
> If you have ever been afraid that hiring would reduce the quality of your service, hiring the right people and giving them the most complete information possible in an employee handbook will go a long way in alleviating that fear.

Much of the training and job expectations that set up your staff members for success are only legally allowed with employees. This is yet another reason that I recommend employees over independent contractors. You simply cannot use an employee handbook with independent contractors.

A Trial Training Period

The best way to train employees (remember: you cannot train ICs) is on the job. Once your new staff members have signed your employment contract and understand the employee handbook (including your company policies and procedures), you can then have them shadow you or one of your top pet sitters or dog walkers for a few visits or walks before doing the visits and walks on their own. This will provide valuable training opportunities if your new staff member needs guidance on how to deal with difficult pets or other common situations that arise on the job.

I recommend that if you are new to hiring, or even in your first few years of hiring, you have the new staff member go with you to three or more client interviews/meet-and-greets. As I mentioned in the chapter on pay, you will need to pay your staff members for the time they spend at client interviews. By the third client meeting, have them run the interview while you simply stand back and observe. After each interview, give them feedback and let them know if there was anything you think they should have done or said differently. If you noticed anything specific that they did really well, point that out, too.

After you are satisfied that they know how to run a client interview, including familiarity with the questions to ask pet owners so they can collect as much information as possible, they can go on their own. A lot of pet sitting business owners tend to go to all new client interviews, but then they wonder why they are so burned out. Hire the best staff members, train them adequately, and then trust them to do their job. If you are micromanaging your staff, you will have even more work to do than you did before you hired in the first place. Plus, having to work around three separate schedules for each appointment is like herding cats. It's much easier to coordinate two schedules (the client's and your staff member's) than it is to find a time when all three of you are available. Setting a goal to have them work towards going on client interviews on their own will save you a lot of time down the road.

Some business owners opt to pay their staff minimum wage during the initial trial period before bumping them up to their regular pay rate. If you do this, be sure it's clearly outlined in the welcome packet and employee handbook so everyone knows what to expect before the very first paycheck.

If you want to improve the training and experience level of your team, you can also support your staff members in getting trained in pet CPR and dog behavior. Your local humane society may have low-cost pet CPR and dog behavior classes available or you could hire a professional local dog trainer to provide private dog behavior lessons for your staff members.

Introduce Staff to Your Current Clients

Many business owners worry about how their current clients will react when they start hiring staff to take over the pet sits and dog walks that they, the business owners, have previously done. That is a normal fear. Your clients may be nervous about the transition, too. They trust you with their pets and their homes, but they don't yet have that relationship with your new staff member.

When it comes time to introduce a new staff member to your current client, be confident going into the conversation. Don't ask your clients if they will be okay with making a switch or apologize in any way. Even if you simply have uncertainty in your voice, they're going to hear that ... and many clients will pounce on that uncertainty to try and keep you.

Be aware that some clients may be upset that you're not doing all (or in some cases, any) of the actual pet care service for them. There is a reason they chose you as their pet sitter or dog walker after all. You have to be really clear with clients, without actually stating it, that this change is not negotiable. Tell them you will still be walking their dogs on Monday, Wednesday and Friday, for example, but that you are no longer available on Tuesday and Thursday. Then tell them that you would love to set up a time for them to meet the new hire you've made and start telling the client what makes your staff member great.

Create a win-win for your clients before you even introduce your new staff members. Let pet sitting and dog walking clients know that your hiring will actually make it easier for them to get appointments last minute and during busy seasons. That way they will see the advantage to them and learn to be happy with the change.

Even though they might be resistant to someone new, it's pretty rare that a client will leave your company instead of working with your new staff member, especially if you have somebody that you stand behind and can highly recommend ... this is where hiring the very best staff members is key. You want to feel great about your new hires so that you can honestly tell your clients how wonderful they are. That enthusiasm will carry through your voice and put many of your clients at ease. They trust you and they will often extend that trust to someone you recommend so highly.

Kristin's Story:

One of the biggest ways to save time in your business is to delegate. Yeah, I know. You may think you know what I'm going to say because everyone talks about the importance of delegation. But the reality is that actually delegating can challenge the deepest desire of business owners — to be in control!

But here's the paradox: If you want more time, you can't delegate some duties to free up your schedule and maintain absolute control of your business at the same time. And so, in the spirit of creating more time and freedom, I recommend spending some time thinking about some of the business tasks that are massive time-suckers and take those off your list by having someone else do them. (I double dog dare you!)

Client interviews can be one of those paradoxical situations for a lot of pet sitters and dog walkers. Many are often afraid to have their staff do the client interviews on their own, and yet they can be a huge time suck when you've got a lot of clients and a lot of staff members. Client interviews can sometimes be a full-time job in and of themselves.

It took me a few years to get to the place of trusting my ability in picking the right staff in order to have them go on their own to client meetings. But once I did, I never looked back. I recommend you do this in your business much sooner than I did!

Hiring Success Stories:

"I go with my new pet sitters and dog walkers for the first five client interviews, and if we both agree they are ready, they go solo after that. I take the lead on the first few new client interviews, and then the pet sitter takes the lead on the rest. During the first five interviews with new clients, I answer any questions the clients may not be sure of, check that all of the forms are filled in, and ask the client relevant questions while the new sitter observes. I explain to pet sitters why we ask certain things, I instruct them to listen for clues to client concerns and pet behaviors, and I offer advice or suggestions. It's important to teach the pet sitters the soft skills when doing client interviews, too. For example, using the client and pet names in conversation, interacting with the pets, wishing the clients a nice trip, and so on."

Sharon Moore - Petcarers Bendigo
Bendigo, Victoria, Australia

"We have always delegated the client meet-and-greets to our staff. Before the sitter or walker meets the client, we do a thorough phone intake initially, so the meet-and-greet is pretty much just that: meeting the client and pets and seeing the 'lay of the land'. Most of the pertinent info (feeding, vet, emergency contact, payment arrangements, etc.) has already been covered during the initial phone call. I do like to tag along to the meet-and-greets when I can, but having the sitters and walkers do the in-person meeting is part of our onboarding/training for new hires."

Becki Bradford - The Pet Company, Inc.
Indianapolis, Indiana

Action Step

Do an internet search for "low-cost background checks", or if you belong to a pet sitter organization, contact them for information on discounted background checks for new staff members. Once you've made an offer to a candidate, start the background check process before they start work.

Action Step

Compile a welcome packet for new staff members that will guide them through the very first steps of working for your company. If you would prefer to purchase a pre-made packet or modify an existing template, you will find my Welcome Packet for the New Staff Member for sale at the website www.SFPSA.com/welcome. The Welcome Packet for the New Staff Member is available for purchase individually or as part of the Hiring Kit for Pet Sitting and Dog Walking Staff at www.SFPSA.com/hire.

Whether you make the packet yourself or use an existing template, be sure to run your documents by an employment lawyer who knows the current employment laws in your area.

Action Step

Using the guidelines in the chapter under "The Employee Handbook", create a comprehensive handbook for employees that contains everything they need to know as part of your business. That way, when they call you with questions, you can direct them to the employee handbook first.

Alternatively, if you would prefer to purchase a detailed and thorough employee handbook template for easy modification, you can purchase one on my website: www.SFPSA.com/employee.

Action Step

Practice notifying clients of your new staff member by calling a friend and having them pretend to be a pet sitting or dog walking client. Be confident and positive and avoid asking permission or conveying uncertainty. At the end of the practice phone call, ask your friend for feedback on how to make the conversation more positive and specific.

Action Step

Take your new staff member to at least three client interviews as a training opportunity. Give your new hire a little more responsibility during each meet-and-greet until you feel comfortable taking a step back and simply observing. When you reach that point, you'll know you can hand over that responsibility to this staff member completely.

ELEVEN

Schedule Staff for Success

How to Best Utilize Your Staff and Organize Their Time

"The key is not to prioritize what's on your schedule but to schedule your priorities."

–Stephen Covey

Every staff member you add to your business complicates the process of coordinating schedules a little bit more. With the tools I will give you in this chapter, that coordination can be simple and straightforward ... rather than a logistical nightmare. Since one of the main benefits to hiring is to free up more of your time and energy for you as the business owner, you'll want to set up a streamlined system that keeps scheduling as easy as possible.

Tips for Successful Scheduling

Before setting your initial staff calendar (or updating one that's already in effect), review these scheduling tips to avoid common potential pitfalls and keep your business running smoothly:

- **Use scheduling software to coordinate staff member's calendars.** A scheduling software program will take much of the work off your plate once you are comfortable using it. Email me at Success@SFPSA.com for my recommendation if you need help figuring out which software to choose.

- **Set up a communication system.** How are staff members going to know their schedules for the coming week? Will you send out an email or text message? Use an online scheduling system that sends automatic reminders? Go ahead and set up a way to share scheduling information with your team now so they know what to expect from day one. Check the *Recommended Resources* section at the end of this book if you want some ideas of apps and programs that make it possible to communicate quickly and easily with your team.

- **Hire enough team members.** Plan on enough dog walkers for each to work no more than two to three days a week (either M/W/F or T/TH) and make sure you have enough pet sitting staff hired well in advance of busy holiday and summer seasons. If you don't have enough staff to cover all your appointments without overscheduling your current staff (or yourself!), you may need to make additional hires.

- **Build the schedule around specific staff.** Instead of simply plugging staff members into available slots, consider the personalities, skills, strengths, and weaknesses of each staff member. If you have staff members that are especially talented or in demand, you can start building your schedule with them. Over time, you may find that you become an expert "matchmaker" of pet care provider and client.

- **Keep drive times to a minimum.** As much as you can, make sure no sitters and walkers are traveling more than 15 minutes to work. (Think in terms of drive time when scheduling, not miles.) The more time a sitter or walker has to spend traveling to and from work, the more likely they are to burn out and end up quitting. Be conscious of that. I've had staff members say they are fine to do long commutes to jobs initially, but when it came down to actually traveling a long distance to work multiple times a week, they didn't want to do it after a short time.

- **Double check for scheduling overlaps.** If you have staff members that do both pet sits and dog walks, make sure they are never scheduled for two jobs at the same time. This is especially important if you opt to maintain separate pet sitting and dog walking schedules. This is where a software system shows its worth once again, as the right system will alert you to double bookings automatically.

- **Honor requests for time off as much as possible.** There will be times when you simply can't give someone the day off they've requested. But by working with staff requests when possible, you will build morale and increase staff satisfaction. This also helps prevent staff burnout—a common cause of high staff turnover. I suggest setting up an online "Absence Request Form" for your staff members. That way, there will be an established method for requesting time off and you will avoid having to remember who asked for which days off in the middle of other business tasks.

- **Let staff members find their own subs — with permission.** If a dog walker needs a last-minute substitute, it will be much less work for you if they find someone to cover the shift themselves. As the business owner, it will be your job to approve the substitution to make sure no one staff member has too many hours and that the person covering the shift is qualified to do so. Be sure the client has given their okay for a substitute staff member to go into their home and walk or visit their dog. What you really don't want to do is get in the habit of being that emergency backup yourself as the business owner. Make it a top priority to require emergency shifts to be covered by other staff members, even if it feels easier to just take care of it yourself.

Covering for sick days and emergencies is not the only way your staff members can make scheduling easier by sharing work. In the next section, you will find another example of how utilizing multiple staff members for the same job can simplify your appointment scheduling.

Sharing Work Between Staff Members

In an ideal world, you'd have one pet sitter or walker for the same client, but that's not always possible. There will be times when multiple staff members will be needed to cover one client's appointments. In these situations, you will want to create as much continuity as possible. First, limit the number of staff members that are sharing a client to as few as possible. With each additional person that works with each client, you will have more oversight work, making sure nothing falls through the cracks. Keeping the client sharing to a minimum will make your clients and their pets more comfortable as well.

How to choose to divide up each client's appointments will depend a lot on whether you have more dog walks or pet sits on your schedule, or vice versa.

For dog walks, the process is fairly simple. If you've followed my suggestion and hired dog walkers for either a M/W/F or T/TH schedule, you will only need two walkers for every client that requests walks every day during the working week. Although you may be able to fill each week's appointments with two walkers, I suggest having at least three staff members trained and comfortable with each dog walk client, if at all possible. That way, if one can't make it and the other is sick or unavailable, the third walker is likely to be able to fill in. As long as you make sure that each walker has the chance to meet with the client and dog(s) before they start, the backup rotation should be easy for everyone to get used to.

If your business is primarily pet sitting visits, on the other hand, there will be more coordination on your part to make sure everything gets done. Setting regular feeding, walking, and medicine administration times will help prevent anything important getting lost in the shuffle between staff. You might consider scheduling one staff member for morning visits and another for evening visits. For very long visits, be sure to alternate weekend duties as well so that no single staff member has to work every weekend. Also, make sure that clients know there will be a three-hour window for sitter arrival times. Having a bigger time window in which the sitter can arrive will make the transition between sitters much easier to coordinate as well as eliminate not being able to keep your word when it comes to pet sitting visit times.

Dealing with Client Keys

As you add staff members to your business, you may need to modify the way you handle client keys to make sure that your staff have access to the home as needed and that your clients' house keys are kept secure.

One easy method for dealing with client keys is to have them stored in a small key lockbox at the client's home. That way, any one of your pet sitters or dog walkers visiting the home for an appointment can access the key. If you choose to use this approach, provide each client with a lockbox at the client interview for a deposit. Then, make sure to include the lockbox code (which either you or the client can decide upon) in the pre-appointment information you provide to your staff.

If you decide to store client keys in your home office, be sure to label them in a nondescript way—do not label the keys with the clients' name or address for their security. How you choose to label the keys is up to you, as long as you can keep track of which key belongs to which client while protecting client privacy. I've seen some business owners choose to label the key with the pet's name for easy reference.

If you store client keys in your office, purchase a large lockbox for storing all of your keys securely, and always have your clients also leave a spare key with a neighbor or nearby friend in the event of a lost or broken key.

Ideally, all staff members that are part of the regular appointment rotation will have a spare key (or easy access to a spare key) of their own. Be sure to have each staff member with access to a key try the key in the door before leaving the client interview. Sometimes spare keys don't work well, or at all. It's much easier to deal with right at the client meet-and-greet than at the first pet visit or walk.

For backup staffing situations, however, you may need to facilitate a smooth and secure handoff of the spare key. A 24-hour P.O. Box or lockbox can make it simple for staff members to exchange house keys in the case of an emergency backup. By storing the key in a secure location (like a lockbox), you won't need to worry about the backup staff member leaving their shift with the key and scrambling to get the key back before the regular sitter or dog walker shows up for work.

Staffing Holidays

Holidays are a hectic time for pet sitting, but it's also not uncommon for many pet sitting staff members to request time off during the busy season. Make sure you have adequate staff in town for holiday appointments by scheduling months ahead. In my own business, for example, I started coordinating end-of-the-year holiday staff schedules as early as late August or September.

Here are a few suggestions for making the process run smoothly in your own business:

- **Discuss holiday availability during the interview.** As I wrote in an earlier chapter, I neglected to ask my first two hires about their holiday schedules and ended up doing all of the end-of-year holiday pet sitting visits myself. You can avoid a similar situation by always checking the Schedule Availability section of the application packet when you are doing the face-to-face interviews and by clarifying with all candidates what their expectations and availability are for holidays.

- **Set a mandatory holiday requirement.** Tell staff members early in the year (at the time of hire, if possible) what the expectation is. I required each team member to work two of the three year-end holidays. That way, everyone got the holiday of their choice off and I still had plenty of staff members available for our busy holiday schedule. Remember that you can't actually require specific shifts of independent contractors, which is yet another benefit to hiring employees.

- **Ask staff members about their holiday requests early.** By starting in late August or September to coordinate holiday staffing, you will have plenty of time to work around each person's requests as much as possible.

- **Split the holiday fee with your staff.** If you charge extra for holiday visits, and I suggest that you do, split that increase with the staff member(s) working the shift. That way, they will feel your appreciation and have something extra to look forward to in their next paycheck to compensate for the holiday(s) worked. I found it was easier to establish holiday periods rather than managing specific days. For example, I set a four-day Thanksgiving period (rather than just Thanksgiving Day) and established one holiday period for everything from December 20th through January 3rd. Go back to Chapter 6 for an entire section on managing holiday pay and fees if you want more specific information about how this works.

Kristin's Story:

When I first began hiring dog walkers to take over my own dog walking jobs, I wasn't thinking about needing backup staff. I was only thinking about how great it would be to get a break from Tuesday and Thursday dog walks. A couple of months later, however, I got a call from one of my T/TH dog walkers that she'd broken her arm and would need to take a break from dog walking for at least eight weeks. Since I had no backup dog walker, I was once again "in the field" and back to dog walking.

I quickly realized that in order for me to avoid being the backup dog walker for future emergencies, I needed to have at least two dog walkers (and preferably three) trained on each dog. I wasn't able to do this right away, but as my dog walking staff grew, I began training as many dog walkers as possible on all the dogs. That way, multiple staff members had met both the dog and human clients so that if they were needed in a pinch, they could easily step in and take over if need be. This served me well and prevented me from being the emergency backup.

Hiring Success Stories:

"Part of how I 'sell' clients on the lockboxes is that I let them know the boxes are theirs to keep and will come in handy if they have guests visiting or construction being done on their home, etc. I buy them in bulk and sell them

for twice the amount I pay. There are so many people with lockboxes on their homes these days, I don't think it's a red flag. For an apartment complex, it's a bit different: The apartment manager agrees to keep keys in the office and the sitter would be required to show ID in order to get the key."

Brandy Nightingale - The Peaceful Pup
Ojai, California

"We have our staff fill out an availability form when we hire them, which includes their holiday availability. We allow everyone to take off one of the three major holidays at the end of the year (Thanksgiving, Christmas, or New Year's) so that they can spend at least one holiday at home with their family uninterrupted. So far, it's worked well for us and a lot of our pet sitters choose to work all three anyway."

Ashley Chidester - Aunty Ashley's Pet Nannies, LLC
Atlanta, Georgia

Action Step

Pick a calendaring and communication system that will enable you to set schedules and notify staff members about their upcoming shifts. Exactly what you need will depend on the size of your business and which features you need. Check the *Recommended Resources* section for ideas or email me at Success@SFPSA.com for my software suggestions.

Action Step

Modify your client key storage, if necessary, to accommodate your new staff member(s) and to make the passing of keys an easy experience. Choose a recommendation from the chapter (lockbox, office storage, and/or 24-hour P.O. Box) and convert clients to that system. Add "test client key" to the client interview checklist to ensure that the key works at the first pet sit or dog walk job.

Action Step

If you don't have a holiday policy yet, set a mandatory holiday work requirement of two out of the three end-of-year holidays for your employees. That way, everyone will know what is expected of them with plenty of time for you to arrange their schedules appropriately.

Action Step

Once you've decided how many end-of-year holidays you need each staff member to work, start collecting time off requests and preferences by no later than September 15th. This will give you the time you need to figure out how many appointments you can reasonably staff and gives your employees plenty of notice so they can make plans.

Action Step

If you haven't already, add a 20% (or specific dollar amount) holiday surcharge to all visits (and walks, if there are any) that fall within the holiday periods you establish, as discussed in Chapter 6 and in the Staffing Holidays section of this chapter. Notify your clients well in advance (or when they book your holiday services) of the applicable dates and rate so that they are prepared for the increase when the end-of-year holiday season rolls around.

TWELVE

How to Keep the Best Staff Members

Avoid Staff Burnout and Show Your Appreciation

"Treat your employees exactly as you'd want
them to treat your best customers."

–Stephen R. Covey

Now that you've gone through the effort to find and hire the very best staff for your business, you'll want to keep them. Staff turnover is an expensive headache for you as the business owner, and it is difficult for your clients, too. Pet sitting and dog walking is a business of relationships; you and your clients will all be happier if your stellar staff stick around long enough to develop those relationships and really contribute to your business over a long period of time.

Even though reading this book and following the *Action Steps* through the process of hiring a new staff member has left you better equipped to hire a replacement now than you've ever been before, your top priority should always be to keep the great staff you already have. After all, you've taken the time to find just the right people to invite into your business, filed the necessary paperwork and (if you have employees instead of independent contractors) gone through the process of training them. Extending effort to keep your current staff happy is always easier than starting again at square one with a new hire.

> **Hiring Tip:**
> Extending effort to keep your current staff happy is always easier than starting again at square one with a new hire.

Hire the Right People to Begin With

This may seem obvious, but there is a reason I keep coming back to it: Hiring the right people to begin with, even if it takes a bit longer to find them, makes everything easier in the long run. Having the right staff will save you time and money — and help lower stress.

All the information and details you get from the application packet will help you identify which applicants are interested in a long-term job and who is just looking for a temporary or seasonal gig. During the interviews, you will also have a chance to evaluate each candidate's goals and overall fit.

Another step you are already taking that will help retain staff members is issuing a very clear welcome packet and employee handbook to each employee. (Remember, if you are hiring independent contractors, you will need to modify the welcome packet to fit the legal requirements for ICs and likely will not be permitted to use a handbook at all.) The clearer you can be with your new staff members about what they will be expected to do while working for your business, the more they'll feel comfortable in their jobs. That comfort leads to higher quality work, fewer mistakes, and happier employees.

In addition to making the best hires from the outset, there are some things you can do to encourage staff retention.

Set Them Up for Success

You can encourage the sort of working environment that pet sitters and dog walkers will want to be part of long term by giving them the best chance for success in these four areas: (1) paying them appropriately, (2) setting the right schedule for each staff member, (3) making it easy for them to love coming to work, and (4) ensuring they have the tools and support they need.

Pay them appropriately.

In the chapter on pay and wages earlier in this book, I recommended that you pay your staff as close to the highest rate in your area as you can to attract the very top candidates. I also described the three-tier pay system I used in my own business, enabling me to increase staff pay as they gained experience and to reward longevity with yearly raises. Go back to Chapter 6 if you'd like to read about either in detail. Remember, employee satisfaction is not all about money, but having a competitive pay structure will help you keep the best employees loyal to your company.

Set the right schedule for each staff member.

When I wrote about staff schedules and calendaring, I encouraged you to give each dog walker a regular schedule of two or three days each week. One of the reasons I recommend this is to prevent burnout. You can set your new hires up for success from day one by making sure they have enough time off to take care of themselves and their personal and family obligations. Also, as dog walking can be a somewhat monotonous job (same dogs, same route, day after day), scheduling a day off between each dog walking day will give your staff a much-needed break and help the job feel more like a fun opportunity than a never-ending chore.

Many times, new hires start out really enthusiastically. They are eager to make money (that's one of the reasons they took the job after all) and are initially excited about most, if not all, aspects of the job. If you aren't careful, however, that enthusiasm can quickly fade when the newness of the job wears off. I found that my dog walkers and pet sitters were not always upfront with me if they were feeling overworked or stressed. They may hint to me about being overworked and then quit suddenly.

When I started paying attention to how many breaks they were getting, I noticed that many of the same staff members that quit suddenly were also the ones who were working many days in a row without much time off. There is no magic number of hours staff members can work before they feel overwhelmed because each person's need for time off is different. I recommend you start by aiming for at least two days off each week. Three is even better. Not only will this give them a chance to recharge, but it will also help you avoid overtime pay.

As the business owner, it will be your job to observe their stress level and time off. Encourage them to practice self-care and provide them enough personal time to take care of their own physical and emotional needs. If you aren't sure how many hours of work each staff member can handle, here's a hint: Their energy and motivation are probably less than half of yours since business owners often have a lot more motivation and passion for the business than employees ever will!

Make it easy for them to love coming to work.

Another factor that contributes to staff burnout is how difficult it is to get to work in the first place. As I mentioned in the last chapter, limit drive time to 15 minutes each way when at all possible. You'll notice that I phrased that in terms of time spent driving, not miles. That's because, as anyone who lives in an urban center knows, travel time depends as much on traffic conditions as it does distance. Rural pet sitters and dog walkers may be able to travel much further in 15 minutes than those covering congested areas. Ultimately, you'll need to adjust the scheduling, staffing, and driving times to fit conditions where you are operating your own business.

I also found that staff members were happier at work if I assigned them jobs they were interested in, when possible. Not every dog walk or pet sit job will be perfect, and it's not reasonable for any staff member to expect only the best clients and easiest pets or jobs. That said, if you know that one staff member really likes active dogs and another feels more comfortable with cats or mellow or aging dogs, use that knowledge to match each staff member with the best client fit when you can. You will also know the personalities of your new hires and your existing clients better than anyone else. Use that knowledge and really think about who will work best together. Both your clients and your staff will be happier when you serve as "matchmaker" and can find a great fit.

Ensure they have the tools and support they need.

No one likes to feel overwhelmed or in over their head at work. This is where a quality welcome packet, employee handbook, and scheduling software come in. Make sure your staff members know exactly what they need to do (and who/when/how to ask for help if they need it) before they start any solo jobs.

Although you don't want to micromanage your employees (and legally can't dictate details of how independent contractors get their work done), you can set them up for success by making sure they have the proper training and resources to feel confident in their job. In the next chapter, I go over how to review staff work to evaluate whether or not their performance is meeting the quality level you expect.

Be Generous

One of the best things you can do to keep team members happy at work is to be generous with your praise. It may sound like an overly simple suggestion, but it is an incredibly powerful part of managing staff. In fact, some studies have shown that being appreciated at work has the biggest impact (even more than pay) on how long an employee will stay with a company.

Express your gratitude when a job is done well. If you notice a staff member going above and beyond or persevering with a difficult situation or client, thank them. People appreciate hearing they've done a good job. Don't wait until the end of the year or a work anniversary, either. Go ahead and tell them you appreciate them right when you notice a behavior or attitude you want to cultivate in your business. If a client emails or calls the office to let you know a staff member has done an exceptional job, take a moment to immediately call the staff member and relay the compliment. I've found it's important to do it right then, even if it means putting your other work on hold. If you put it off, you may forget.

Another way you can show your staff that you appreciate them is by giving them the chance to provide input into how the business is run. Give stellar workers the chance to make suggestions if they have an idea that can improve the company. You may be surprised at the good ideas they come up with. They may also appreciate the opportunity to learn a new skill or take on more responsibility after they've been with the company for a while. This shows them that you value their efforts and want them to be around for a long time.

Generosity can also be financial. Gradually raising staff wages and occasionally offering bonuses and extra time off can really improve morale. Even though you will be spending money to reward them for a job well done, financial generosity often saves you money as well. Happier staff members do a better job and are less likely to quit, saving you the time, money, and energy it would take to hire a replacement.

You are not the only person who can or should be generous with your staff. Have you ever considered encouraging your clients to show their gratitude as well? It can be as simple as adding something to each reservation confirmation that says, "Tips not required but welcome". Doing so doesn't require much from you but it can really make a difference. When I added that line to my own confirmations, I saw an 80% increase in client tips for my staff.

> HAPPIER STAFF MEMBERS DO A BETTER JOB AND ARE LESS LIKELY TO QUIT, SAVING YOU THE TIME, MONEY, AND ENERGY IT WOULD TAKE TO HIRE A REPLACEMENT.

Kristin's Story:

As I mentioned earlier, one of the biggest gifts you can give staff is to pass on appreciation from clients. In the beginning of my hiring journey, I would get client appreciation emails and calls praising certain staff members. After receiving the praise, I would think, "I'll contact the staff member later today to let them know the client loved the work they provided," but inevitably a business task would come up and I would forget. Soon it would be a few days or weeks later before I remembered and would tell them thank you from the client. Although the pet sitter or dog walker would be very grateful for the praise, the appreciation was much less relevant and meaningful because it was so delayed.

I realized that I really needed a better system of relaying this information in the moment rather than days or weeks later. I began to think about client praise as a tennis game. When the client "lobbed the praise over the net", I needed to return the ball by contacting the pet sitter or dog walker in the moment rather than letting a pile of "praise balls" gather dust behind me. When I turned the process into a game ("I need to lob this praise ball over the sitter's or walker's net"), it helped me do it in the moment.

Hiring Success Stories:

"Here are six of the most important things I've learned over the years:

1. I make sure pet sitting or dog walking notes are consistently updated for the client each time staff does a visit or a walk.

2. If a dog walker is taking over a dog walking client, I'll have them shadow the existing walker for hands-on details about the dog.

3. I give all staff members their own work email so communication is separate from other aspects of their life.

4. I double-check their schedules to make sure they can get to everyone within the given time (as we get bigger this is time consuming but still worth it).

5. I try to assign clients to staff I think will be the best fit. Example: If we get what sounds like a 'high-needs' client, I won't introduce them to a staff member who I know can't handle the extra detailed work.

6. I set boundaries so staff doesn't get pushed into bending backwards for clients."

Stephanie Surjan – Chicago Urban Pet
Chicago, Illinois

"I have left jobs for a position that paid less simply because of bad management and/or not feeling appreciated. Sometimes you win and get good pay with good management! Unfortunately, that's not nearly as often. It doesn't even take much appreciation, just managers treating you like a fellow human being and not just another cog in the wheel that makes a big difference."

Brienne Carey - BC Pet Care
Wheaton, Illinois

"Recently we gave an employee a 25-cent raise per visit. It's not a lot but every little bit counts. Each employee gets a vacation bonus on his/her work anniversary. It's an average of one week of pay for that year. We randomly give a bonus check (typically after a heavy work period) or a gas card or Visa card. For Christmas, everyone got a Yeti and some simple things (Hot Hands, hand cream, foot cream, ChapStick, rain poncho and Starbucks card). Our long-term employee also got a gift card for a massage at a local yoga/massage studio.

I also offer verbal and written praise frequently, provide continuing education for which they are paid, seek their opinions, and forward the praise reports that clients give in the software system."

Beth Leatherman Harwell - Dog Walkers & More at Coddle Creek, LLC

Mooresville, North Carolina

Action Step

Look through the four ways you can set staff up for success listed at the beginning of the chapter under "Set Them Up for Success". Are there one or more areas that could use improvement in your business? Perhaps changing the way you schedule staff or improving your welcome packet and employee handbook so the duties are clearer. Jot ideas in your hiring success journal so you will have them written down if and when you decide to make a change.

Action Step

Be generous with your praise. Commit to finding at least one positive attitude or act to compliment a staff member on this week. You may be surprised at how much of a difference that compliment makes. Also, make a commitment to pass on praise from clients as soon as you get it. Stop whatever you are doing and call or email the staff member to let them know how much the client appreciated the service they provided.

Action Step

Start saving now for holiday gifts and staff bonuses. Set up an automatic savings plan (if your bank offers one) to put some money aside each month to use at the end of the year or whenever you plan to give gifts or bonuses.

Action Step

If you don't already have it, add a "tips welcome" line to your software system and website. This will help clients who aren't sure what's appropriate and will be another way you can show your staff that you value the work that they do.

THIRTEEN

Manage Complaints from Staff Members

How to Deal with Problems and Issues That Arise with Your Team

"To win in the marketplace, you must first win in the workplace."

–Doug Conant

Once you expand your business to include staff members, the nature of your job will change. While you may be handling clients and taking some pet sitting or dog walking jobs yourself, you will also be responsible for managing your new team members as well. A large part of running a team is balancing the needs of each staff member with what is best for the business as a whole.

I already wrote about showing gratitude and keeping the best staff members happy in your business, but even with those practices in place, I've never met a business owner who didn't occasionally need to address issues between staff members or specific staff complaints. In this chapter, I will tell you how to deal with problems as they arise and what you can do to prevent them in the first place.

> A LARGE PART OF RUNNING A TEAM IS BALANCING THE NEEDS OF EACH STAFF MEMBER WITH WHAT IS BEST FOR THE BUSINESS AS A WHOLE.

Transparency Prevents Staff Discontent

A lot of problems can be avoided from the beginning if you communicate clear company policies and stick to them. Many of the policies that will keep your staff members happy at work should be outlined in the welcome packet and employee handbook. (As discussed in the earlier chapters, remember that these items should only be given to employees and not to independent contractors. Independent contractors have more freedom in how they complete their work and can't be required to follow a handbook or checklist.) For example, if you plan to raise pay rates after six months or give higher wages to long-term employees, go ahead and explain that you do that to promote loyalty. If they are ICs and you've already factored in mileage to their rate, be sure to tell them.

Starting new staff members off with knowledge of what to expect while working for your company prevents the majority of complaints before they even start. (Go back to Chapter 10 if you want to review the welcome packet and employee handbook information again.)

Another step you can take to prevent issues from growing out of control is to encourage staff members to come to you with problems. To avoid a constant stream of complaints, however, set up a system for them to report issues or make suggestions. This might be a dedicated time each month to have a phone meeting or a specific reporting system so they know they will be heard, and you don't have to put out constant complaint fires all day long. I cover regular employee performance reviews in Chapter 15 if you want more detail.

Hiring Tip:
Starting new staff members off with knowledge of what to expect while working for your company prevents the majority of complaints before they even start. (Go back to Chapter 10 if you want to review the welcome packet and employee handbook information again.)

What to Do When a Team Member Complains

When a team member comes to you with a complaint, try not to immediately dismiss the issue or get defensive. Even if you ultimately change nothing about the way you run your business, it is important for staff members to feel like they can come to you with issues.

When a staff member approaches you with a complaint, assuming they've followed the procedure you've outlined in your business policies, answer the following questions to formulate your response:

1. **Is this a valid complaint?** Take a look at the issue from your staff member's point of view. Do they have a reason to feel discontent? Can you understand why they feel this way? If you aren't sure whether or not the complaint is legitimate, calmly ask your staff member for more information so you can better understand the issue.

2. **Have you heard this complaint before?** Some employees are just prone to complaining, but if you hear the same thing from multiple employees, there is probably a valid reason. If more than one staff member has come to you with a similar issue, it should be a sign to you that the problem is larger than you might have realized. In fact, if more than one person has the same complaint, chances are good that other team members are also experiencing a similar issue or are thinking the same thoughts (but just haven't said anything to you about them yet).

3. **If the issue is between two or more staff members, have you heard from all parties?** There is always more than one side to any story. Before you decide how to proceed with the complaint, make sure you have talked to all parties so you have all the information from the very beginning, rather than assuming the first staff member to bring it up is right. (I explain how to deal with staff/client conflict in an upcoming chapter.)

4. **How difficult would it be to make the change your staff member wants?** If you determine that the complaint is valid or seems to be important to multiple staff members, take the time to really consider what changes would be necessary to resolve the issue. Would you need to increase your pay rate? Will hiring more staff members allow you to give your staff more time off? Can you change staff assignments around to alleviate the problem between staff members or staff and a particular client? Be honest with yourself about what you can and are willing to change.

Once you've answered these questions and evaluated the issue thoroughly, you can decide whether or not to make a change in your business practices or scheduling. Even if you decide not to make a change, be sure to respond to the staff member who brought up the complaint and let them know why you decided not to make the change they wanted. Doing so will validate your staff member's feelings and help them understand your perspective.

I hear about some of the same staff complaints from my coaching clients year after year: gas prices, not enough or too many work hours, dealing with difficult clients (or pets), and pet sitter or dog walker burnout. Each of these complaints can be addressed following the four-step procedure outlined earlier in this section.

When Staff Members Leave

One of the concerns I hear from business owners is that their unhappy staff members will end up leaving the business and taking clients with them. They feel like they have to choose between making a change they do not want to make or losing their clients.

I wrote about this issue in an earlier chapter, and to clarify further, here is what I tell my coaching clients who have this concern: Most of your staff members have no desire to start and run their own business. They do not want to do all the work that you did (and still do) to get a business up and running and keep it running smoothly. However, if you hire many people in the course of your business, there may be one or two who do leave to start a pet business of their own. That can be painful, but it is not as common of an issue as some business owners believe.

Some businesses choose to include a non-compete clause in their employee contract, but be aware that non-competes are expensive to enforce (court costs, etc.) and sometimes they will be null and void in court anyway since state and local laws vary so much. It is difficult to know if your non-compete clause will hold up in court without the advice of a local employment attorney. Go back to Chapter 10 if you want to review my suggestions for employee contracts and need more information about non-compete clauses. The bottom line is this: Don't worry about your staff members leaving to start their own businesses. If you are doing your best to take care of your staff, clients, and business, most situations can be resolved without losing your precious clients and staff.

Don't Underestimate the Impact of a Chronic Complainer

Have you ever known someone who could always find something to be unhappy about, no matter the situation? I have, and they always manage to bring down the mood of events and activities by constantly pointing out the negative. Just like chronic complainers can ruin a social function, they can also have a significant negative impact on your business.

You might be tempted to ignore a chronic complainer, hoping the issue will simply resolve itself, but doing so comes with a risk. Their constant complaining may spread negativity throughout the entire team and breed discontent, making your job harder and more stressful than it needs to be.

Since dog walking and pet sitting are primarily solitary duties, your staff members will most likely not have a lot of interaction with each other. Even still, there are more ways a chronic complainer can hurt your business than just breeding negativity among the staff. For starters, you will probably get very tired of listening to their constant complaints. Remember that one of the major goals for hiring in the first place is to relieve some of your stress, not add to it. In addition to tiring you out with complaints, unhappy staff members may also start complaining to your clients, which is yet another reason you should do what you can to reduce negativity and complaining among your staff as soon as possible.

What can you do about a chronic complainer? First, speak to the staff member alone and let them know that you do care about their thoughts and experiences in your business, but that constant complaining is not the best way to get their needs addressed. Give them the opportunity to talk about what is bothering them in a constructive way. Once you have heard their issues and made a decision about how to proceed, how they react is up to them. If their negativity continues, you may need to consider letting them go for the good of the company. I write more about the process of letting employees go in the next chapter.

Kristin's Story:

When I first hired dog walkers and pet sitters, I would find myself either getting annoyed by complaints from my staff or ignoring them altogether. Over time, as I became a more experienced and skillful boss, my perspective changed. I realized that although they didn't seem like it at the time, the complaints were gold — I gained so much from each complaint when I took the time to really understand what my staff member needed.

If I ignored complaints or simply listened but didn't address them, the staff member who made the complaint would, understandably, often leave in a few weeks or months. If I listened and actively worked to try and solve the issue that was causing the complaint, the staff member felt heard, respected, and appreciated. These staff members would bend over backwards trying to do the best job possible and would end up staying with me for many years.

That said, there were also staff members who were "chronic complainers". I had to prevent the excess complaints by setting up a specific time of the month to discuss complaints instead of scattered all over the day, week, or month. That dedicated time, as well as the other examples I've given in this chapter for those who are constant complainers, made a big difference.

Hiring Success Stories:

"I had an employee who complained about the times I assigned her pet sits and found something to whine about on too many visits. For example, she didn't like the time between visits, and she complained about the number of pets or extra work at any visit. If she had a dog walk in the morning and was assigned another in the early afternoon, she didn't like that either.

In addition to her constant complaining, she took an excessive amount of time off for long vacations. Since she was my first employee, she knew a lot of my clients and their pets since she was assigned a lot of visits. When she took time off, it was like being solo again. I had to manage a growing business as well as all the visits in the field. She also wanted to take off time when I was at an annual pet sitting conference.

After a couple of years of this employee's demands and complaints, she became more of a drag than an asset. By now I had enough staff to train on every pet household, so I wasn't scrambling for coverage. I gradually started fading her out of more and more assignments and she eventually retired.

She was a good first hire for me. She enabled me to handle my increasing client base and she gave me a chance to practice my "boss" skills. She taught me the importance of being a decisive leader. Most of all, she changed my mindset about what to look for in the new hire process. I used to think that the best candidate was someone who knew a lot about animal handling. Now I place attitude above skills. I have an excellent training program for the latter."

Jeanne Crockett - Crockett's Critter Care
New Bern, North Carolina

"Sometimes the best way I've found to handle complaints is to see for myself what is going on. We were hired for potty breaks for three small dogs and did that for many months. After some time, the client added two guinea pigs to the home but did not ask us to care for them. A few months later, the cages started to smell. You could tell they hadn't been cleaned in quite a while and they were out of food and water. My pet sitter, out of the goodness of her heart, would provide fresh food and water and sometimes hay. The problem continued and then the bugs, gnats, flies started appearing.

When my employee started complaining about it, I personally took one of the visits so I could evaluate the situation. It was so disgusting! I reached out to the client with a kind heart, offering to add an additional visit so that we could clean the cages for them, and I offered to meet a pest control company rep at the home for her. She took a week off and made a few changes. A few months later, the conditions were bad again. After two notices, I finally told her that we were no longer a good fit and would not be able to service her any longer. Our hearts broke for the pets, but I couldn't subject my employees to that any longer. It was the right move. We are a professional company and do not condone neglect of pets for any amount of money."

Christi Phillips - Posh Paws Pet Care
Summerville, South Carolina

Action Step

Evaluate your welcome packet and employee handbook for transparency. Could a staff member who has questions about pay raises, time off, or other benefits easily find the answers in the information they've been given? If you aren't sure, have a staff member or friend review the documents and provide feedback. Edit the documents to include any necessary information. Then, notify all current staff members of the change.

Action Step

Establish a system for staff members to communicate their complaints or concerns. Do you want them to contact you on the phone, in writing, or in person? Notify your staff of the policy so everyone is on the same page. If you decide that email is your preferred method, for example, tell your staff that they can direct questions or concerns to you via email at any time. If it's not included already, add the policy to your new hire paperwork and employee handbook so all of your new hires have up-to-date information as well.

Action Step

In your hiring success journal, practice answering the questions outlined in the "What to Do When a Team Member Complains" section of this chapter. If you need a few ideas of sample complaints to address, here are some common issues among small business employees: 1) gas prices going up, which makes driving to work more expensive; 2) another team member keeps promising shift trades but not keeping their end of the deal; or 3) staff not feeling like there is room to grow/earn more over time.

Action Step

Set your timer for 15 minutes (or more, if you have a large business) and spend that time evaluating your staff members one by one. Do you have any chronic complainers on your team? Is there a staff member that is especially helpful or hurtful to the morale of your staff or the overall mood of the company? If you identify any chronic complainers, find a time to meet with them individually to discuss their concerns and attitude, and set up a regular monthly meeting to address future concerns.

FOURTEEN

How to Let Staff Go

What to Do When You Have to Terminate a Team Member

"Dealing with employee issues can be difficult, but not dealing with them can be worse."

–Paul Foster

Even with the most careful interview and hiring process, you will eventually need to say goodbye to some of your staff members. It is never easy to fire a staff member, especially if you like the person, but it is a skill all business owners need. In this chapter, I will explain how to know when it's time to let someone go, how to go about it, and some specific legal requirements you need to know. Remember that only employees can be fired. Independent contractors have very different job terms. As a result, most of this chapter will focus on letting an employee go, although you will find a section on terminating contracts with ICs at the end of the chapter.

How to Know Someone Isn't a Good Fit

Only you can decide if and when it's time to terminate a member of your staff. There are too many variables involved in each individual pet care company and group of employees for me to give you one hard and fast rule about firing. That said, there are some common signs it may be time to let someone go.

The more of these that apply, the more likely it is that you need to start the termination process:

- You find yourself doing their job often, either because they aren't showing up or because they aren't doing it well enough.

149

- Their actions do not reflect the values of your business (honesty, kindness, punctuality, etc.).

- They seem to thrive on drama and are constantly having problems with other staff or clients.

- You have had multiple clients complain about them or the quality of their work.

- They've lied to clients or to you.

- They keep missing shifts without adequate notice or finding a substitute.

- They violate company policy, even after you've brought the issue to their attention.

After reading through the list, do any of your employees come immediately to mind? If so, it might be time to consider ending their employment with your company. Very rarely does waiting to terminate a problem employee improve the situation. An employee causing the same problems over and over again is unlikely to change. If anything, more time makes things worse.

> VERY RARELY DOES WAITING TO TERMINATE A PROBLEM EMPLOYEE IMPROVE THE SITUATION. AN EMPLOYEE CAUSING THE SAME PROBLEMS OVER AND OVER AGAIN IS UNLIKELY TO CHANGE. IF ANYTHING, MORE TIME MAKES THINGS WORSE.

How to (Gently) Let Them Go

Firing is not a particularly pleasant thing to do under any circumstances, but there are some steps you can take to make sure it goes as smoothly as possible for you and for the employee you are letting go:

Give warnings first. Before jumping straight to firing, give your staff member a chance to fix whatever is preventing them from succeeding in your business. In many cases, bringing an issue to their attention and giving them the support or training they need to improve can sometimes be enough to resolve the issue.

1. **Keep thorough records.** Any time you give directions or warnings to your staff, keep track of what is said and when. That way, if it does come to termination, you will have a "paper

trail" to show that letting them go was for work-related reasons and not any form of discrimination.

2. **Always do the actual firing in person.** Once you decide firing is the only option, meet with the staff member in question in person. "Breaking up" with someone by text or on the phone hurts a lot more than doing it in person. It's the same with your employees. Not only does meeting in person show more respect to your staff member than terminating them via email or phone call, but it is also much easier to avoid misunderstandings when you can both see each other and rely on non-verbal communication instead of just what is said. Don't take the easy way out. It is poor leadership to fire them over the phone or via email.

3. **Consider inviting a witness.** If there is any chance that your employee might feel slighted or wronged in the firing process, having a third party in the meeting can provide a witness for you in case of a dispute.

4. **Secure company property and client keys the very same day.** If possible, don't let them leave the meeting with anything you need back from them. It can be very difficult to track down items from a terminated employee. They may have hard feelings or simply be busy at a new job, both of which can make it hard to get in touch with them to get the needed items back once they leave. In addition to recovering physical property, you will also want to protect the business's digital property. If your fired staff member had access to admin software systems or company email, be sure to revoke their access and/or change the applicable passwords.

6. **Assume the rest of your staff will hear about what you say.** News travels fast. It's safe to assume that at least some of what is said will be common knowledge among the staff before long, so choose your words carefully. Even though the staff member you let go may decide to tell other team members about it, you should always be sure to keep details of firing meetings between you and the staff member being let go, out of respect for their privacy and to protect yourself legally.

7. **Be clear, but kind.** Be clear and concise, just like you are with your clients. Show kindness, concern, and respect, but don't give your employee the impression that you are temporarily suspending them or giving them a choice about leaving if you know you're not. Even while you are being clear, you will want to be as kind and gentle as possible. If you are willing to give your employee a positive recommendation in the future, go ahead and tell them that now. Ending on a positive note will help you both feel better.

Your Legal Responsibility

Federal law prevents employers from firing employees due to discrimination (firing on the basis of age, sex, disability, race, or religion), for whistleblowing (complaining about illegal activity, safety violations, or harassment in the workplace), or for taking legal leave (time off for jury duty or family leave). Be sure that when you decide to fire an employee, you have documentation to show why you're taking that step in terms of job performance so there is no room for a lawsuit. If you have any questions about whether a particular behavior constitutes terms for firing, consult an employment attorney before beginning the firing process.

Another important detail to discuss with an attorney is to get clarity on what your contract can say about terminating employment. An employment lawyer can review your contract with you and let you know what you can and can't do in the firing process based on the contract you and your employee both signed. Links to staff contracts available for purchase and low-cost attorney options are listed in the *Recommended Resources* section at the end of the book.

Not all states require you to give terminated employees their final paycheck immediately, but many do. Check with your state labor laws by contacting your state department of labor or a local employment lawyer so you know when you have to pay your employee their final wages and still be within the legal requirements in your area.

Terminating Independent Contractors

You can't fire an independent contractor. That isn't to say you are stuck with your independent contractors forever. In cases where the work is not meeting the contract requirements, you can choose to end your working agreement. It will be up to you to provide evidence that the contract terms are not being met, however, so documentation will be key. Be sure the evidence you compile is objective (not dependent on any one person's opinion) so that there is no room for a judge to disagree with your evidence.

As long as the contracted work is being completed within the terms of the contract, however, you can't terminate an IC contract until the contract is complete without incurring whatever penalty is agreed upon in the contract (if there is such a penalty mentioned at all). Again, you will want to be very clear about what your contract says about terminating the agreement *before* you cancel a contract with an IC, so contact an employment lawyer if you need help reviewing your contract. This is one reason I strongly recommend hiring employees instead. You give up quite a bit of control when you utilize ICs instead of employees.

Some states require that you give the IC the chance to fix the work before the contract can be terminated. Again, this is something that a local employment lawyer can help you determine for your area and business.

Kristin's Story:

In spite of having hired over 250 pet sitters and dog walkers in the course of my 18 years of owning my pet sitting and dog walking business, I (thankfully) rarely had to fire staff. But when I did, it was a decision I made thoughtfully and often talked it over with a trusted adviser and an employment lawyer. This was to make sure that firing the person wasn't a reaction but rather a well-thought-out and conscious decision. It's not something you'll want to do lightly, either.

Getting fired is like breaking up with someone, and rejected people are likely to feel ashamed. Ashamed people sometimes react poorly by retaliating, which is yet another reason you'll want to be very careful when letting someone go. Think of how you let difficult clients go — very gently. In the same way, you want to fire people with the same gentleness you'd use when placing an egg on the counter. Dropping an egg will make a mess (and a smell if it's not cleaned up thoroughly), and so can firing someone if it's not done as carefully!

Hiring Success Stories:

"I had a staff member who was upset after she found out how much I charged clients versus how much she got per walk. She demanded 75% of the fee or she would leave. After I stopped laughing, we agreed to part ways."
Stephanie Sorensen - Zen Dog, LLC
Norcross, Georgia

"When a staff member did a 30-minute visit that turned into three hours, I got a call from the client at 2:30 am. Her doorbell camera showed my staff member leaving with a kitchen trash bag full of something and several cans of food in her arms. After checking to be sure the dogs were fine, I accompanied the police to the helper's home, on the insistence of the client. After searching her car, police found the bag. It was full of empty food and drink containers! Turns out the girl was suffering from anorexia and bulimia (which doesn't show up on a background check). She had practically cleaned out the client's pantry and then purged it all out during her three-hour stay. She was removing the empty containers to hide what she did and to replace it the next day. When I talked to her about it, she denied all of it at first. Once that trust was gone, I couldn't continue working with her."
Ginger Young - Jazzy Jack Pet Care Services, LLC
Aurora, Colorado

"I had to fire someone last summer for not showing up. The GPS showed that she had been to the client's. But when I billed one client she told me that her dog had been at boarding all week while she was on a business trip. The client suggested I check with the boarding facility, which I did. After that, I started following the employee. She would go to the client's house, pull into the driveway, and sit in her car for half an hour before driving away."
Josie Hamel - Pets R Us Pet Sitting Services, LLC
Little Elm, Texas

Action Step

Read through the "How to Know Someone Isn't a Good Fit" section at the beginning of this chapter. In your hiring success journal, write down any additional points that feel like justification to fire someone. You'll want to know what behaviors are not acceptable and which can be corrected before the situation arises so you'll be able to deal with it more effectively.

Action Step

Go back and read the "How to Know Someone Isn't a Good Fit" section one more time, as well as any additions you've made in your hiring success journal, considering your current staff while you read. Do you have any problem employees who seem to fit multiple points on the list? Are there any borderline problems that you'd like to correct before things get worse? Is it time to let this person go?

Action Step

Set your timer for 15 minutes. In your hiring success journal, make yourself a firing checklist using the information from the chapter. What will you need to have on hand for an employment termination meeting? Where will it be? Who will be there? You can use this checklist to make sure you are prepared when the time comes that you need to fire an employee.

Action Step

Review your employee contract (or individual job contracts if utilizing independent contractors) and employee handbook with an employment lawyer. Ask for specific guidance on anything you need to know, do, or avoid when it comes time to terminate an employee or end an IC contract.

Action Step

If you have any current employees or independent contractors that are hurting (rather than helping) the business, it may be time to let them go. Using the resources in this chapter and the information you prepared during the previous *Action Steps*, meet with your staff member and end the business relationship.

FIFTEEN

Protect Your Business Reputation

Monitor Staff, Address Client Complaints, and Review Staff Performance

"An ounce of performance is worth pounds of promises."

–Mae West

Earlier in this book, I encouraged you to release your fear of not being in control so you could hire the very best staff for your business. Although giving some of the responsibilities of the business to your staff is a great step toward more time and freedom for you, you will obviously still want to protect the good name of your business. This chapter is all about making sure your team members are doing their jobs, mediating staff and client conflict, and making sure the reputation you've worked to develop for your business lasts, even when you expand to include a much larger team.

Hire the Right People and Prepare Them to Succeed

The two most important actions you can take to earn positive reviews and maintain a stellar business reputation are to (1) hire the right people and (2) prepare them to succeed with adequate training and resources. Hiring will almost certainly take longer, and you will have more work to do getting each new staff member started, but all that time and effort will pay off quickly. Rushing through hiring and/ or training almost always leads to jobs completed poorly, higher staff turnover, and unhappy clients when the job is not getting done right.

If you aren't 100% positive that you've hired the right staff members and given them the tools and information they need to do their jobs the way you want them done, go back through this book and fill in what you may have missed. Even if you've already made it through hiring, it's never too late to refine your process and notify current staff of any new policies. Many of the earlier chapters in this book are dedicated to finding just the right person for the job and making sure your new hire packet, employee handbook, and onboarding procedures are detailed and thorough.

Regular Quality Assessment Protocol

In addition to being deliberate about how you grow your team, it's important to keep track of what and how your staff members are doing on the job. The first part of quality control is to monitor your staff at work.

Here are five ways I suggest you monitor your pet sitters and dog walkers without actually following them around on the job:

1. **Have staff members check in and out.** At the beginning and end of each job, have staff members notify you either through voicemail, email, or by using features of a dedicated pet sitting and dog walking administrative software system. Whichever method you choose, make sure there are timestamps tracking when the call was made or the email sent. For more experienced staff, you may choose to only have them contact you after the first and last visits in a particular pet sitting assignment or on the first day of a regular mid-day dog walking job.

2. **Monitor staff locations during assignments via GPS.** Specific app suggestions for GPS monitoring are included in the *Recommended Resources* section. Also, some pet sitting and dog walking administration software systems have GPS tracking for staff built right in.

3. **Give each employee a thorough checklist of what should be done at each walk, visit, or overnight.** Remember that you cannot legally give a checklist of duties or instructions to an independent contractor, however, so this suggestion is only for employees.

4. **Make occasional visits to staff jobs.** If you feel there is a reason to do so, stop in during an appointment and see how your pet sitter or dog walker is doing on the job. Doing so can alleviate the stress you might feel about how a new hire is working out. If you choose to visit your staff on the job, be sure to tell your staff from the very beginning that you may stop in and see how assignments are going. Otherwise, they may feel like you don't trust them to do their job.

5. **Conduct formal performance reviews for employees every three to six months (for new employees) or yearly for longer-term employees.** This performance review will give you a chance to discuss how the job is going from your staff member's perspective and to talk about anything that needs to change. When possible, you will want to use direct quotes from client satisfaction surveys—more on that next—to give examples of a job well done or something that could be improved.

Client Satisfaction Surveys/Questionnaires

Client satisfaction surveys (or questionnaires) are one of the most impactful ways you can keep tabs on how your staff members are doing on the job and what clients think about your business.

Client surveys will give you a peek into the day-to-day appointments handled by your staff and provide you with specific feedback to use in their performance reviews. In some cases, like with great feedback, you might also share that feedback the very same day you get it. In an earlier chapter, I explained how sharing positive feedback immediately with staff bolsters morale and gives your team members motivation to keep doing a good job. At least some of these compliments from clients will come from their client surveys.

It is worth noting that I have found a much greater response to specific satisfaction surveys than just waiting for clients to contact me with feedback. This is likely because people are more willing to write down feedback on a satisfaction survey than they are to pick up the phone and call you unless they are really upset about something. If you only rely on the customer phone calls and emails that come in spontaneously, you will probably assume that fewer clients are satisfied or displeased with the service than is accurate. Most satisfied and mildly dissatisfied clients are not motivated to contact you and share what they like (and don't) about your staff's performance. Asking for regular feedback through a client questionnaire is a great way to get a more accurate view of how your clients really feel about your staff and your service.

There are a number of ways to send and receive satisfaction surveys. In my experience, I get many more responses from clients when I use paper questionnaires they return in the self-addressed, stamped envelope I provide. I think this is because people are more willing to sit down and write about their experience than they are to fill out an online survey, visit a website, or make a phone call. Online or text message surveys can be useful for quick feedback, but the number of responses I receive back—as well as the detail of their reviews—has always been much higher when I use mailed surveys with a self-addressed, stamped envelope provided.

That said, depending on your client base, you might choose from any number of survey options: sending an email questionnaire, giving each client a physical survey (complete with self-addressed envelope), or utilizing survey software or apps to create a survey that clients take online or via text message. How you conduct satisfaction surveys will depend a lot on the way you run the office side of your business. However you do it, send a questionnaire to all clients at least once a year and to new clients within the first week of their first appointment.

Hiring Tip:
Online or text message surveys can be useful for quick feedback, but the number of responses I receive back—as well as the detail of their reviews—has always been much higher when I use mailed surveys with a self-addressed, stamped envelope provided.

Staff-Client Disputes

No one likes to have unhappy customers, but most pet care business owners have learned, with experience, how to listen to customer complaints and fix the problem(s). When the complaint is directed at one of your staff members, things get even more complicated. Is the customer really always right when it comes to staff-client disputes?

When I first hired staff members for my own business, and a client called with a complaint, I nearly always assumed the client was right and my staff member had been in the wrong. In reality, this was the exact opposite of what I should have done, and I quickly learned to contact the staff member immediately after hearing from the client in order to get both sides of the story. Always give your staff the benefit of the doubt. You've been very careful in selecting and training them, after all. There could be a good reason they did whatever it is your client perceived as being wrong. If you jump to conclusions and accuse your staff before you know all the facts, you may end up losing both the client and the staff member!

IF YOU JUMP TO CONCLUSIONS AND ACCUSE YOUR STAFF BEFORE YOU KNOW ALL THE FACTS, YOU MAY END UP LOSING BOTH THE CLIENT AND THE STAFF MEMBER!

When a customer calls or emails with a complaint, it is up to you as the business owner to juggle both the desire to make things right with a client and the need to back up your staff members so they feel your support.

With those opposing objectives in mind, here is how I suggest you handle customer complaints:

1. **Listen.** Talk to the client and get as much information as you can without taking a side, assigning blame, or apologizing (yet). Express empathy without placing blame on either the client or the staff member. End the conversation by telling the client that you will get back to them soon with a solution.

   If you have a hard time talking to people when they are upset without getting upset or feeling defensive yourself, here are some questions and phrases you can use to keep the conversation moving: "What happened next?" "Start from the beginning, please." "Help me get up to speed." "Will you repeat that last part?"

2. **Talk to the staff member(s) involved.** Follow the same procedure with your staff member. Do not blame or take a side, but do get as much information about what happened as you can.

Keep the discussion focused on "just the facts, ma'am" when emotions get high. That will help the conversation be as positive and proactive as possible.

3. **Offer a solution.** Once you've had the chance to evaluate what happened, contact the client with a solution. There may be times where you determine that your staff member did nothing wrong, so the solution may be as simple as explaining what happened (and why) more fully to your client. There may be other situations that require changing which staff member is assigned to this particular client moving forward, providing the next service at a discount, or refunding the entire cost of the service when the problem happened. It can sometimes be a good idea to let your staff member propose how to fix the problem if you think they can do so without making things worse.

    When you tell them how you've decided to solve the problem, focus on what you *can* do for them instead of telling them what you *cannot* do. You may not have every option or be willing to do what the client wants completely, but there is always something you can offer.

4. **Document any relevant information.** I recommend that you have staff files for all your staff members where you can write down what happened, the date of the complaint, and how you dealt with it. If you do end up needing to fire the staff member involved, this documentation will be important to show you had a legitimate cause to terminate their employment.

5. **Figure out what went wrong.** What led to this situation that could have been prevented? If your staff member has done something wrong, it is a reflection on you and how you've hired and trained your staff.

    Take a hard look at what your part was in the conflict:

- Did you leave something out in your instructions to them?

- Did you not educate or train your staff properly?

- Did you fail to communicate (or instruct them to communicate) adequately with the client so they would know what to expect?

A good leader is someone who can see and admit what they haven't done well. Answering these questions after a complaint arises will help you improve as a business owner and prevent similar problems in the future.

6. **Follow up.** Soon after the conflict is resolved, follow up with both the client and the staff member(s). Make sure that everyone feels their issues have been addressed. This will also give you an opportunity to retrain staff that may not have been taught correctly and to communicate clearly with clients whose expectations may not have been in line with the reality of the service your business provided.

Kristin's Story:

As I mentioned in an earlier chapter, I made the mistake early on in my business of assuming an upset client was always right instead of asking staff their version of what happened. This caused me to lose a couple of really great staff members. When it happened the second time, I had a good staff member quit due to my unwillingness to ask for their side of the story. I had to learn from my mistake so I didn't keep repeating the unhealthy and damaging pattern.

When you are on the receiving end of an angry client email or phone call, I really encourage you to take a big breath and not jump to conclusions. It can be easy to instinctually take your client's side and assume your staff was at fault. Be sure to take the time to talk to your staff member. Yes, you may lose a client if you can't resolve the situation the way they want, but ultimately, if it wasn't the staff member's fault, you don't want to be out a client *and* a staff member. In the long run, I've found that a good staff member is often more valuable than most individual clients.

Hiring Success Stories:

"When I first hire a new staff member, I do at least 10 new client intakes with them to make sure they fully understand the process. I follow up with all clients on a regular basis to make sure everything is done to their expectations. Our sitters call, text or email us on the first day of each new assignment and when the duration of the service is longer than one week, they contact us once per week with an update. I also start training sessions with all new hires to go through complete pet sitting instructions, first aid, and common animal illness symptoms."

Anja Gangur - Fido & Feline Holidays and Daycare
Guelph, Ontario, Canada

"I have my new staff go on many visits, as well as client consults, with me. Ideally, I get them to the point where they can work without me having to babysit them. It is a work in progress but so worth it. I have one gal who has been with me 10 years, so as soon as I give her the new client info, I know she will take care of it all and I never worry."

Julie Graves - Julie's Pet Sitting
Corona, California

"We let the client know they will receive a photo and a text (or email if going overseas) on the first visit to let them know the visits have started, all is well, and a brief update. Clients love it. Especially the photo! Nothing beats real evidence that your pet is okay."

Sharon Moore - Petcarers Bendigo
Bendigo, Victoria, Australia

Action Step

Choose how you will monitor your staff during their appointments, whether that means having them call to check in and out of each walk/visit or by utilizing some combination of administrative software and GPS monitoring. Check the *Recommended Resources* section for specific suggestions and then dedicate at least 30 minutes to learning how to use all the features of any new GPS app or software you decide to use.

Action Step

If you don't have them already, create detailed checklists for each type of appointment your staff will handle (dog walks, overnight visits, etc.). Alternatively, you can find premade versions of each of these checklists in the Welcome Packet for the New Staff Member for sale at the website www.SFPSA.com/welcome. As another option, it's included in the Hiring Kit for Pet Sitting and Dog Walking Staff at www.SFPSA.com/hire. All purchased checklists from the website can be edited and customized for your particular business needs.

Action Step

Schedule regular performance reviews with your staff. If you haven't been conducting dedicated quality checks, you'll want to meet with each staff member right away and then every three to six months for newer team members and every year for those who have been with your business for more than a year. If you are dealing with any chronic complainers, you may need to set up regular monthly reviews for a time so they can discuss their concerns more often.

Action Step

Create a client satisfaction survey/questionnaire for all clients and a variation of the same survey to send new clients within a week of their first visit or walk. Check the *Recommended Resources* section at the end of this book for specific apps and software that can help you create and administer your client surveys.

SIXTEEN

Hire Help for the Business of Running a Business

Bring on Office Assistants, Accountants, and Other Professional Help

"You can do anything but not everything."
–David Allen

When you first started reading this book, you were probably looking for staff to help you take on some of the dog walks and pet visits. I've written about the hiring and training process for pet care employees throughout the book, but the benefits of hiring exceptional people don't stop at pet sitters and dog walkers. Some of the best help you can hire for your business may come from administrative assistants, accountants, bookkeepers, lawyers, and more.

Office Managers vs. Administrative Assistants

One of the most common questions I get from coaching clients is whether they should hire an office manager or administrative assistant. First off, there is no hard and fast rule as to what classifies someone as an office manager versus an administrative assistant. That said, there are a few specifics that tend to differentiate the two positions.

Here are a few of the traditional differences and why I recommend hiring an administrative assistant first:

- **Administrative assistants handle the day-to-day office work.** Office managers usually train and manage employees, as well.

When you first hire help for the office side of your business, you will probably want to continue to select, train, and manage each employee yourself.

- **Office managers generally make more money than administrative assistants.** Although I don't suggest you make hiring decisions based on salary alone, it is important to consider the cost of both employee types. If you advertise for an office manager position, many of the applicants will be expecting a higher pay rate than you may be willing (or able) to give at this time.

- **Office managers often have degrees in business administration.** One of the reasons office managers tend to garner a higher wage is that they have spent time and money to earn a degree specifically targeted toward office management.

When you get to the point in your business where you are ready for someone to manage your staff and run the business without you being present every day, it will be time to hire an office manager. In the meantime, an administrative assistant will provide daily support while still deferring most personnel and management decisions to you.

The Power of a Great Office Manager or Administrative Assistant

One of the best things I did in my own business was to hire outstanding office assistants. During the years I owned my business and regularly traveled abroad, I had as many as five office assistants running the business while I was out of the country for months at a time each year. They did a wonderful job and I am so grateful for them because they were one of the important keys to my freedom. Are you wondering how to find equally capable help for your business? If so, read on.

First, you will need to create a job description for this position. What is it that you want your assistant to do? To answer this question, think about everything you, as the business owner, do in a day in addition to dog walks and pet visits. You answer phone calls and emails, schedule new client interviews, update the dog walk and pet sitting schedule, order office supplies or schedule repairs, and handle all the important situations that can crop up without warning. A skilled administrative assistant will be able to handle all of these things and more.

The regular duties of an office manager or administrative assistant include everything it takes to keep your business running smoothly day to day.

THE REGULAR DUTIES OF AN OFFICE MANAGER OR ADMINISTRATIVE ASSISTANT INCLUDE EVERYTHING IT TAKES TO KEEP YOUR BUSINESS RUNNING SMOOTHLY DAY TO DAY.

The best office managers and administrative assistants will:

- **Return all client calls and emails courteously and promptly.** This requires a certain level of tactfulness and organization that not all potential employees will have.

- **Verify that all staff check in and out of scheduled pet sitting and dog walking jobs.** If anyone has not checked in or out on time, they will call the staff member to see what is happening and deal with any issues that have arisen.

- **Email you a "phone and email log" after each shift.** I found that receiving a daily log of calls and emails from my office assistant was very helpful so I could keep tabs on what happened each day and promptly address anything that needed my attention when I was back in the office.

- **Contact you in the event of any emergency they can't handle on their own.** You will want to decide which situations you want to hear about right away and which you want the office manager/administrative assistant to handle on their own. Be sure to add that information to your office assistant training manual, which I write about in the "Training Your Office Manager or Assistant" section later in this chapter.

- **Schedule appointments for new and existing clients.** Although it may be a couple of months before they are ready to handle scheduling responsibilities, you will eventually be able to give them control over scheduling. That way, they will be able to accurately price the services and know which sitters are available when.

From that list alone, you can probably already see how useful it will be to have the right person helping around the office.

How to Find the Right Office Manager/Administrative Assistant

When it comes to hiring an office helper, it is easiest to hire someone who is already working for you as a pet sitter and dog walker. Here's why: They already know how your company operates and are familiar with your services and pricing. They understand the ins and outs of what dog walking and pet sitting entails, which is especially beneficial if you give them any management or training responsibilities. They may even be able to take on pet sitting and dog walking appointments as needed. If you do have an office assistant who is in charge of scheduling and also accepts shifts themselves, be sure that they are scheduling appointments fairly for all staff and not "cherry picking" the very best clients for themselves.

My best administrative assistants and office managers started off as pet sitters or dog walkers for my business. Because of that experience, they knew both sides of the business. They were able to run the business in an efficient way because they understood exactly what went into each service we provided, the administrative needs of the business, and the perspective of the employees they were helping to manage. That being said, just because they have worked in your company and have been a great dog walker or pet sitter does not mean they will make a great office worker, since office work requires a very different skill set than pet care. You will want to follow the same selection and application process for all potential office assistant/manager candidates, even those who are already working for you in another capacity.

If you don't have any current pet sitters or dog walkers (or don't have any who are a perfect fit for the office assistant or management position) and want to hire an administrative assistant, you will need to look outside your company to find someone for this role. Some of the pet sitters and dog walkers I've coached have even had success in hiring a client who has the right experience and personality for the office job. Whether you advertise online or just approach someone you know who could be a good fit, be clear about what you expect a successful administrative assistant to handle and how many hours it will take each day/week.

In order to be able to have clear expectations in your job posting, start tracking your own hours now for a full month or two to get a sense of the different tasks your administrative assistant will need to complete and how many hours that will take.

You will find a few time-tracking apps and resources in the *Recommended Resources* section at the end of the book. You can expect that it will take your administrative assistant a few more hours than it takes you to do what you do each week. Since you've run your business for a while, you can get things done much more quickly than someone who is brand new to working on the office duties specific to your business.

Look for an office manager or assistant that has applicable work experience, is friendly with clients and staff, has a track record as a good communicator, can demonstrate organization and efficiency, has the ability to write with good grammar and spelling, and is able to calmly handle emergencies with common sense.

> **Hiring Tip:**
> Look for an office manager or assistant that has applicable work experience, is friendly with clients and staff, has a track record as a good communicator, can demonstrate organization and efficiency, has the ability to write with good grammar and spelling, and is able to calmly handle emergencies with common sense.

Training Your Office Manager or Assistant

Many administrative assistants work from their home, but you will want to train them in person if you can. If they don't live in your area, you can use Skype or another video calling service to do "face-to-face" training online. Doing in-person training makes the training go faster and also helps you determine if you've found the right fit. I suggest hiring your administrative assistants with a trial period of three months so you can see how they manage the unusual situations that are bound to come up now and then.

As you did when training your pet sitting and dog walking employees, you should provide a job manual for your office manager or assistant. The manual should function as both a training tool and reference book for your office assistant to use when questions arise on the job.

I had so many clients ask me for specifics about how I trained my own office managers that I created a comprehensive guide and customizable manual for the office duties. You can find a link to the Office Manager/Administrative Assistant Manual's product page in the *Recommended Resources* section of this book or by going to this link: www. SFPSA.com/manager. If you prefer, you can create your own office manager or office assistant manual.

If you decide to make a manual from scratch, be sure to include these important details:

- The daily and weekly job duties of your office manager/ administrative assistant.

- Detailed descriptions of all daily and weekly duties.

- Login information to your administration software system as well as login to your business email and voicemail systems.

- Answers to common questions that arise on the job.

- A specific statement about when they should contact you instead of taking initiative and handling a situation on their own.

- An acknowledgement form that your office manager/ administrative assistant signs showing that they have read and understand the company policies contained in the manual. This may provide legal protection for you if there is ever a dispute. You may find your manager manual needs to be updated from time to time. Whenever you make a change, you will need to have your office manager/administrative assistant sign a new acknowledgement form that they have read and understand the changes.

It may be second nature to you now, but remember that some of the issues that occur in your business will not be easy for your new administrative assistant or office manager. Be patient, but also thoroughly evaluate their responses for signs of clear thinking, good customer service, and honesty. Your administrative assistant will be representing you and your company, so it's incredibly important that the fit be right.

Other Help for Your Business

Dog walkers, pet sitters, and a great administrative assistant will make up most of your employees, but what about other help your business needs?

Here are some other types of hires you may consider for one-time or ongoing help:

- **An accountant you can trust.** An accountant can help you with the financial aspects of your pet sitting and dog walking business, such as saving for and filing tax returns, making decisions about how to spend your capital, and budgeting for business expansion or liability. It's just as important to find a "people person" you can work with as it is to find an expert on numbers. Look for an accountant who explains things in a way you can understand and who answers your questions without making you feel like an annoyance.

  Once you find an accountant you want to work with, make an appointment as soon as possible. Some of my coaching clients don't start thinking about taxes until early April or wait to start looking for an accountant only when they have an urgent accounting need. That is *not* when you want to be interviewing potential accountants! The best accountants will probably be too busy with existing clients to take on a new business late in the tax season, so find and hire your accountant early.

- **A bookkeeper or payroll company.** If you don't want to manage your own bookkeeping or payroll, hire it out! As with all hiring decisions, you will need to weigh the time and energy it will save you with the money it will cost to pay someone else. If it's worth it to you to let someone else handle the bookkeeping, just be sure to find a reputable company you can trust. Even if you do hire a bookkeeper, it is your responsibility to carefully review the statements and make sure you understand exactly where the company's money is going.

- **An employment lawyer.** I absolutely recommend finding a local lawyer that specializes in employment or small business law to help you with any questions that arise as you continue on your hiring journey. Why a local attorney? The reason is that many employment regulations vary by state. You want a lawyer who will have the most accurate information for your location and situation. If you can't find a local attorney you trust (or who has time to take you on as a client), make sure that your long-distance or online law firm is familiar with your state employment laws. Most online firms will assign you a lawyer who is familiar with the specific laws in your state. For online legal help I recommend, see the *Recommended Resources* section at the end of this book.

Kristin's Story:

It was a few years into my business when I knew it was time for me to hire an office assistant. My initial thought was to place a help wanted ad for the position, but then I realized how much easier it would be to hire a pet sitter or dog walker who was already working for me.

Before I began considering who among my staff might be a good fit, I first wrote a list of all the qualities I wanted my office administrative assistant to have, including: a high level of skill in communicating with staff, clients, and me; common sense; initiative; the ability to handle emergencies that arose; the know-how to troubleshoot, and how best to handle emergencies without assistance from me.

The next thing I did was create the Application Packet for Office Manager/Office Assistant and the Manager Manual. Even though I'd given an application packet to all my dog walkers and pet sitters when they first applied, I knew I wanted to have them fill out an application packet specifically for the office position because this was an entirely different role.

Next, I wrote a list of names of possible office assistants from my current pet sitter and dog walker list. There were three people I felt would be a good fit. Although one wasn't interested in the position when I approached her with the idea, the other two were very interested. After I had them fill out the application packet, one was clearly the right fit (although I still did a face-to-face interview with her before letting her know I'd chosen her).

She was great in her new office assistant role, and having her on board enabled me to have a lot more time and freedom than I'd previously had when I'd been the sole office person!

Hiring Success Stories:

"I have a virtual receptionist who handles my calls Monday through Friday from 8 am to 6 pm. I have found it pays for itself in new clients! I was always letting my phone go to voicemail because it was never a good time for me to answer (hands full!), and a lot of times I'd get caught off guard and not be ready to talk to a new potential client. Not many people leave messages on voicemail; they just move on to the next pet care provider number on their list. Now my receptionist answers the phone from her own location and gives them basic info, takes down detailed messages, and assures them I will call back the same day. It's a nice system and definitely takes some pressure off me."
Lauren Molino - Canine Concierge, LLC
Parsippany, New Jersey

"We call our office manager a 'Client Happiness Leader', and she has been a game changer in our business and quality of life! I went through pregnancy, a long delivery, and now I will finally fulfill a lifelong dream of traveling the world with my family ... all while my business runs in two different locations. How is this possible? Kristin's Pet Sitting Office Manager Manual clearly defined the job and what was needed. It is truly my secret weapon."
Natasha O'Banion - Walk with Renzo and Ruby, Inc.
Washington, DC

"I hired an office manager and she is making all the difference, all because of Kristin's webinars. The most difficult part is getting over that I need to do it all myself (that's still a work in progress). Thank you, Kristin!"
Susan Gibbons - Sara's Legacy Pet Sitters/Dog Walkers, LLC
Traverse City, Michigan

Action Step

Write a list of all the administrative tasks you complete in an average week or month. You can find a basic list at the beginning of this chapter in the section entitled "The Power of a Great Manager or Administrative Assistant" to give you some ideas.

The tasks you do each week may seem easy and obvious to you, but having a written list will be helpful when you sit down to create a clear job description for your administrative assistant or office manager.

Action Step

Continue to track your administrative duties and the hours they take over the course of the next month, as I recommended earlier in the chapter. Add to your list of tasks all throughout the month until you have a comprehensive list to use for a job description in the job posting and manual for your office manager or administrative assistant.

Action Step

Using the list you completed in the previous *Action Steps*, identify which of the duties you'd like your assistant to handle each week. Next, estimate how many hours those responsibilities might take your new hire each day, remembering to include extra time as it will probably take them much longer than it takes you.

Use that list (and the time requirement) to create a job posting and application packet for hiring an office manager or administrative assistant. Or if you prefer, you can purchase a premade Office Manager Hiring Kit which includes an office assistant/office manager job posting, application packet, and manager manual which you can customize for your business needs at www.SFPSA.com/manager.

Action Step

If you don't already have an accountant for your business, make a list of two or three that you think might be a good fit. If you don't have anyone specific in mind, try asking other small business owners in your area or local friends and family. Remember to select an accountant who is good with numbers *and* with people. Avoid condescending accountants or any who seem to be rushing you through the appointment. You want to choose someone you feel calm and comfortable with so you feel at ease when discussing important business issues.

Next, set up interviews with potential accountants. Be sure to give yourself enough time before your tax deadlines to find and hire the right accountant. Establishing yourself as a client early on will allow you to ask your accountant's advice on any tax-related or financial hiring or business questions from here on. Hiring your accountant early will also give you plenty of time to communicate about budgeting for taxes long before they are due so you can avoid unhappy money surprises at tax time.

Action Step

Rinse and repeat! Repeat the third and fourth *Action Step* with any other business hires you need to make, including a bookkeeper or payroll company (if applicable) and employment lawyer in your area.

SEVENTEEN

Master the Art of Delegation

How to Give Responsibility to Your Staff to Create More Freedom and Time for Yourself

"I don't have a problem with delegation. I love to delegate. I'm either lazy enough, or busy enough, or trusting enough, or congenial enough, that the notion of leaving tasks in someone else's lap doesn't just sound wise to me, it sounds attractive."

–John Ortberg

Delegation starts with the internal process of releasing control. For many small business owners, letting someone else take over part of the business can sometimes be uncomfortable. All the way back in Chapter Two, I wrote about releasing your fear of letting go. Many of the techniques in that chapter can help you overcome any remaining fear you may have about delegating responsibilities to your staff. You can refer back to that chapter – and especially the *Action Steps* – any time you want more help pushing through your fear of giving up control. In addition to the information in Chapter Two, the specifics in this chapter will guide you through the process of knowing what to delegate and how to do it step by step.

The Delegating Mindset

The first step to delegating is preparing yourself mentally to let go of some of your control when it comes to running your business. And since it has been rare for me to meet a pet business owner that hasn't experienced at least some discomfort around giving even partial responsibility to someone else, you are probably feeling some of that discomfort, too. For me, it really came down to having the courage to delegate responsibilities in spite of the fear I initially felt doing so.

Here are a few other steps you can take to get yourself in the best mindset for delegating effectively:

- **Hire the right people.** I keep coming back to this point because it really is the best thing you can do for your business long term. Every aspect of delegating responsibility is easier and more effective when you know, in your gut, that your staff members are great and can handle what you are asking them to do. There may still be some initial discomfort when you delegate tasks, but you will feel more peace and confidence if you are sure you've hired the right people for your business (and, if you feel great about who you've hired, you'll also be able to more easily "sell" your clients on your staff members, too).

- **Think long term.** Delegating is a little bit like goal setting; both are more powerful when you expand your vision past what needs doing today or this week. Some tasks might be faster to do yourself than to give to a staff member ... if you're only looking at today's to-do list. Once you consider the task long term, you may realize that you do not want to be the one handling this particular responsibility a month from now, let alone this time next year. That realization will give you a reason to take the time to delegate now, even if it does take a little bit more time and effort than simply completing the task yourself.

- **Establish a priority system for tasks.** If you don't already, learn to prioritize to-do items when you make your daily, weekly, and monthly plans. Rank your tasks three ways: by order of importance, by order of urgency, and by how much skill or finesse they will take to complete. The items with the highest rankings in any category will stay on your plate (for now, at least), while the items lower down on the lists are the first ones you should give away. Learning to prioritize your to-do list will help you make the most out of your days as well as help you decide what to delegate and what to do yourself.

- **Ask the right questions.** Evaluating responsibilities that can be delegated is easiest when you ask yourself thoughtful questions. For example, "When does this need to be done?" "Who can get this done?" "What information or training is needed to get this done?" "How often does this need doing?" The more routine something is, the more it's worth training someone else to do it. Asking yourself the right questions will help you find clarity as you make these decisions.

Once you are in the delegation mindset, it's time to do the actual work of delegating.

Hiring Tip:
Learning to prioritize your to-do list will help you make the most out of your days as well as help you decide what to delegate and what to do yourself.

How to Delegate

I often get questions from pet business owners who are finally ready to give more responsibility to their staff members but aren't sure how. If you've never had to delegate tasks before, getting started can feel daunting ... but it doesn't have to be.

When it comes to actually delegating responsibilities, here are five steps to follow:

1. **Make room in your schedule.** One of the main reasons small business owners don't delegate, other than fear of losing control or losing clients, is that many tasks are simpler and faster to do themselves than to teach someone else how to do them. Because they are unwilling or unable to devote the time needed for delegation and training, they never let go of those tasks. To avoid falling into this cycle, make it a point to set aside time for delegation in your schedule by giving yourself a specific block of time each week to make delegation decisions and complete any of the tasks outlined in this chapter. Scheduling a specific timeframe for delegation helps you make sure it actually gets done.

2. **Pick the right tasks for the right staff member.** By the time you've evaluated their application packets, interviewed each candidate, and trained each new hire, you will know your employees very well. If you are using independent contractors, you will probably also have a decent idea which ICs are ideal for which task after you've worked with them for a while. Use your knowledge of each staff member and their skill sets when you decide how to delegate responsibilities. They will have more success and fewer complaints with tasks that match their skills and interests ... and, as a result, you will be called in much less often to fix problems.

3. **Communicate, in detail, what you expect.** When delegating responsibility, be clear in your instructions so that you and the staff member have the same understanding of exactly what you're expecting them to do. One step I recommend pet business owners take in preparation for delegation is to make a list of everything you personally do when you are actually completing the service or task you plan to assign out to someone else. Make a list of exactly what that service entails. A lot of the time, we are on autopilot when we're doing something we've done hundreds of times before rather than thinking in terms of how to clearly communicate the steps to someone else.

   When you are on a dog walk, it may seem like a simple task, but there is so much more going on than meets the eye. For example, you have to be sure you have the key in your possession and that you don't leave the house and lock the key inside. Tracking each action you take throughout the service can be as easy as keeping notes on your phone while you go through your regular process. Taking notes on what you do will slow you down a little, but it will also help you make a clear and complete job description or task list when you delegate that responsibility.

4. **Set a deadline and follow up.** While the goal of delegation is to move tasks off your schedule to allow you more time for yourself and for nurturing your business, it will still be up

to you to keep tabs on what your staff are doing. Establish deadlines when applicable and schedule a time to follow up and see how the work is going. You will need to check in more regularly with staff taking on new responsibilities—maybe as often as right after the first appointment or task—but you can follow up less frequently with more seasoned staff.

Checking in with team members taking on new tasks will give them an opportunity to ask questions, give you peace of mind that everything is going well, and allow you to celebrate success or fix problems when needed.

5. **Use the Five Stages of Delegation to troubleshoot problems.** Most problems with delegation come from giving too much responsibility too quickly without enough follow up or training from you. When issues arise, it may be because you have rushed through a step in the process.

As a result, I've detailed the five stages delegation takes to get you from completing the job or task yourself to your staff member handling it on their own:

> **Realization:** First, you must realize what specifically needs doing. This is where the list of each step involved in the task comes in.

> **Observation:** Next, your staff member will simply observe what you do to complete the job or task. If possible, give them the task checklist to review while they watch you go through each step.

> **Collaboration:** The third stage of delegation is to complete the job or assignment together. This is a stage that many

managers and business owners neglect when they try to rush to the point where staff members are doing all the work. Even if it's brief, be sure to work through the job together with your staff member. Doing so will give you valuable training opportunities you might otherwise miss.

Evaluation: Before you leave your staff member to work alone, take a step back and watch them handle the task completely on their own. Resist the urge to offer any feedback until the end, if possible.

Delegation: Finally, your staff member is ready to take on the assignment alone. You will still follow up from time to time, but you know from the previous stages that they can handle every aspect of the job duties without you there.

I've included a graphic of the five stages for you to use when you sit down to evaluate how a staff member is handling new responsibility and to figure out where you are in the process (and which step is coming next):

Five Stages of Delegation

I DO	Realization
I DO, YOU WATCH	Observation
WE DO	Collaboration
YOU DO, I WATCH	Evaluation
YOU DO	Delegation

With each new staff member and each delegated task, you will need to work through the five stages in order. That way, you can be sure that every responsibility you delegate is being completed to your satisfaction.

Mistakes to Avoid

As with any other aspect of running a business, delegation takes practice. You probably will not find the right balance of oversight and letting go right away. You may need to monitor particular staff more closely than others or continue to release your fear of giving up control, as I mentioned in "The Delegating Mindset" section of this chapter, in order to find the right level of delegation for your business. That said, by learning from the experiences of other business owners in similar situations, you can avoid many common delegation mistakes.

Here are a few common mistakes business owners encounter with delegation and how to avoid them:

- **Avoid micromanagement.** Resist the urge to hold the reins too tightly once you've given an assignment. Mistakes will happen, but your business will survive them — and you and your staff will all learn from the experience. Refer back to Chapter 15 for information on monitoring and reviewing staff performance, but be aware that watching over staff members' shoulders can harm the trust between you and use up the time and energy you're trying to gain by delegating in the first place.

- **Don't try to solve every problem yourself.** Part of preparing staff for greater responsibility is giving them the tools and resources they need to solve their own problems. At first, they may come to you with everything, but you really need to teach them how to handle small issues on their own. Instead of answering every question or fixing every problem right away, turn the question back to the staff member asking for help. Ask, "What do you think will help in this situation? Have you checked the employee handbook for ideas?" Not only will asking questions save you from putting out every fire, but your staff will also learn to think for themselves and thrive with extra responsibility and trust.

  One of the most common causes of burnout I see among pet business owners is stepping in as the backup pet sitter or dog walker when the regular sitter or walker calls in sick or goes on vacation. Don't fall into that trap! Go back to the "Sharing Work Between Staff Members" section in Chapter 11 if you need suggestions on how to arrange a system where staff members cover for each other instead of relying on you. Any effort and time you put into establishing that system will be worth it in the long run. You simply cannot be the backup option for your staff.

- **Don't give every task to the same person.** You may have one or two staff members you trust more than the rest. Maybe they have worked for you the longest or just seem to get it better than the others. Be careful not to overload them with every delegated responsibility, however, or you will be scrambling to fill their shoes if/when they eventually leave your company ... and they may leave your company sooner rather than later if they get burned out! Extending opportunities to newer staff members will help them improve on their own abilities and enable you to build a network of capable help you can turn to when you have additional tasks to delegate. You will be more able to position your business to run without you if you gradually grow it to include a few (or even many) staff members that can easily handle many responsibilities instead of just leaning on one talented employee.

In "The Delegating Mindset" section of this chapter, I encouraged you to prioritize tasks before deciding what to delegate and what to keep for yourself. You can use a similar system to assign tasks to multiple staff members. A good rule of thumb is to make a list of who can complete a given task and then assign it to the lowest person on your list. If you keep delegating every responsibility to your best team member, you will not give others the chance to improve and grow.

Kristin's Story:

Delegating tasks and jobs can bring up a lot of emotions for the delegator! I've seen uncomfortable feelings surface in my coaching clients many times as they have stretched beyond their comfort zone and hired people to help them. My advice for those who are afraid is to "feel the fear and do it anyway."

Delegating is not going to feel comfortable until you build the "delegation muscle," which only happens with practice. As business owners, we only have so much time, energy, and bandwidth to take care of both the mundane and important tasks that require our attention in any given day. When we delegate some or even most of our daily tasks, we gain more freedom and time, and can then become the visionaries of our company, instead of the "worker bees."

> DELEGATING IS NOT GOING TO FEEL COMFORTABLE UNTIL YOU BUILD THE "DELEGATION MUSCLE," WHICH ONLY HAPPENS WITH PRACTICE.

Hiring Success Stories:

"I am having one of my pet sitters who has been with me for over three years do office work, such as scheduling visits, canceling visits when appropriate, answering phones – general office stuff. She doesn't do anything involving the financial end of things. Even though I trained her for a few weeks, it was pretty scary to let go. We met, talked a lot, and worked together over the phone until I felt more secure that she knew what she was doing. Now I am able to have her cover and get some time off to work on business and enjoy my personal life, so it was worth it. I am also confident she will ask if she has trouble with anything."
Sandy Getchell-White - Purrfect Place for Pets, LLC
Charlottesville, Virginia

"I hired a CPA because I have absolutely no interest in that side of the business. They file all of our taxes and do our payroll for a very reasonable monthly fee."
Stephanie Sorensen - Zen Dog, LLC
Norcross, Georgia

Action Step

Set your timer for 15 minutes. In your hiring success journal, write down what a normal month of work looks like for you. Create a bulleted step-by-step list for each task you complete in a typical month. Evaluate what parts of your current workload you imagine doing a year from now. Which items do you imagine being a staff member's job instead? Use this list to figure out which tasks to delegate first.

Action Step

If you haven't already, prioritize your to-do items this week by importance, urgency, and how much skill is required to complete each task. With practice, this will become second nature to you when you sit down to make your to-do lists each day or week. Doing so will help you as you delegate responsibilities to your staff because you will be able to easily decide which tasks are best kept for yourself and which should be given to other staff members.

Action Step

Schedule a time this week to delegate at least one responsibility to a staff member. Follow the steps in the "How to Delegate" section of the chapter to choose the right task, the right staff member, and the right way to communicate what needs to be done. Add delegating time to your weekly or monthly schedule. This will enable you to regularly assign new tasks and follow up on previous assignments.

EIGHTEEN

What Hiring Will Do for You

Enjoy the Professional and Personal Benefits of Hiring Exceptional Employees

"Great vision without great people is irrelevant."

–Jim Collins

At the beginning of the book, I promised you that hiring exceptional staff members would bring powerful benefits to your personal and professional life. If you've been thoughtfully reading each chapter and working through the *Action Steps*, I hope you have discovered many of those benefits already. And if not, I encourage you to take the time to go back and complete each *Action Step*—they have been specifically designed to help you apply the lessons from each chapter to your own hiring journey. As you read through this chapter, ask yourself which of these benefits you're seeing already and which you are still hoping to find. Doing so will give you an expanded vision of what hiring will do for you and motivate you to continue to grow your business and prepare your staff to work independently. I've broken down the advantages that hiring brings into two categories (professional and personal), but most small business owners know better than anyone how interconnected your personal and professional lives really are.

Benefits for the Business

Hiring exceptional staff members to assist with dog walks, pet sits, and office work will enable your business to grow more than you might have thought possible. Most pet business owners who have thoughtfully hired the right staff end up experiencing more positive benefits from hiring than they ever expected.

Here are a few ways that hiring will help your business thrive:

- **You will have time to work *on* the business instead of *in* it.** Think of all the work you'd like to do for your business that isn't the actual pet sits and dog walks. Hiring staff will free up the time you are now spending doing pet sitting and dog walking, giving you a lot more time to answer emails, implement new or improved marketing strategies, and handle client issues as they crop up without struggling to fit it all in before and after a full day or week of pet care.

- **You can take on more clients and expand the reach of your business.** With additional staff members, you will be able to accept more business instead of having to turn valuable new clients away. In all my years of business ownership, I've discovered this truth: When I create space for growth and new business, it always comes. Sometimes you have to take that leap of faith to make room for more success.

- **Your business will have a true visionary and leader — you.** An empowered leader does more than just hire, schedule, and manage staff. When you've been in business for a number of years, your business will benefit from you being at the helm with an eye on the long-term instead of stuck in the day-to-day trenches. Intentional, regular goal setting is crucial for any business. A clear company vision can make business decisions easier because every choice will be pointing to an overarching mission. You will have the time and energy needed to create that vision, inspire your team and plan for the future of your business when you have the staff to handle a lot of the other work.

> IN ALL MY YEARS OF BUSINESS OWNERSHIP, I'VE DISCOVERED THIS TRUTH: WHEN I CREATE SPACE FOR GROWTH AND NEW BUSINESS, IT ALWAYS COMES. SOMETIMES YOU HAVE TO TAKE THAT LEAP OF FAITH TO MAKE ROOM FOR MORE SUCCESS.

Even with all the growth and increase that hiring will bring to your business, those benefits pale in comparison to the positive changes you will see in your personal life.

Benefits for You

In the very first pages of this book, I told you about how draining my business was for many years. I was overwhelmed and burned out, and I didn't see any relief in sight. Hiring exceptional staff was a major part of rediscovering time for my personal life and goals outside of my business. Joy and energy came back into my life and reminded me of what was really important to me other than the running of my business.

You may have already started to feel some of that renewed joy yourself as you find time to do the following:

- **Take time off when you are sick or need a break.** When was the last time you took time off from your business? If you're like most small business owners, it's very rare, and you are probably still working from home on your "day off." If you haven't started to take advantage of the ability to leave the business behind for a few days, schedule a long weekend and rediscover what it feels like to turn off your phone and have a true day off.

- **Focus on personal relationships.** Relationships take time and energy, and you have probably been short on both while you started and grew your business. Now that you've hired some help, make time for the people in your life who have taken a backseat to your business. Go on vacation together, enjoy a lunch date *without work distractions*, or whatever relationship building you've felt like you could never do because of work.

- **Be creative.** Creativity takes energy, but it also generates energy as well. You will find incredible power and regeneration in picking up a new hobby or revisiting a favorite activity you haven't had time for recently. Music, visual arts, dance, and making time for playfulness will improve your quality of life (and, as a bonus, make you a better business leader as well).

- **Travel.** One of the very best results that came from my hiring exceptional staff for my business was the ability to travel. I still spend a lot of time traveling abroad... and love it! If a similar life speaks to you, start working towards it. Take weekend trips as often as you can and start planning to leave the business for a few weeks this coming year. Each time you travel, your staff will handle your absence a little better, become more adept at solving challenges that arise while you are away, and you will reap the many benefits that come from stepping away from work to visit new places regularly.

Hiring Tip:
Taking care of yourself with the same dedication that you give to your clients and your business will help you avoid burnout and give you the stamina you need to reach your personal and professional best.

Practice Regular Self-Care

Self-care is the practice of actively protecting your own health, well-being, and happiness. Self-care is incredibly important, especially for business owners, because you are giving so much of yourself to the business each day. Taking care of yourself with the same dedication that you give to your clients and your business will help you avoid burnout and give you the stamina you need to reach your personal and professional best.

Practicing regular self-care is crucial to business success and should be done at least every week. You wouldn't keep putting off car maintenance or medical care just to cross more items off your to-do list. Why not? Because you know that the longer you wait, the worse the problem may become — and the more time and money it will take to make it right. Self-care should be as important. There's a saying about meditation that if you're too busy to meditate for 10 minutes, you should meditate for 30. Self-care is similar. You may think you don't have time to take care of yourself right now, but if you don't, you will be forced to take the time later when you are sick, burned out, and completely drained of energy.

In the *Action Steps* at the end of this chapter, I encourage you to form a habit of regular self-care starting right now. Possible self-care actions include anything that you deliberately do to improve your emotional, mental, and physical health.

Here are some ideas you can use to visualize what self-care looks like in practice:

- Schedule time in each day for exercise and meditation.
- Treat yourself to a massage or pedicure.
- Get enough quality sleep, whether that means going to bed earlier or finding a way to unwind before bed, so your sleep is deeper and more restful. Put down or turn off any screens (yes, even your smartphone!) at least two hours before bed for the most relaxing sleep possible.
- Take yourself to a movie you've wanted to see.
- Eat good, nourishing food that you enjoy and that fuels your body well.
- Have lunch with a friend without checking your phone or multitasking during the meal.
- Find something that makes you laugh, whether that means going to a comedy show, watching a funny movie, or spending time with friends.
- Set a time to be done with work for the night and build in more relaxation and rest in each evening.

Your self-care will not look like anyone else's because what renews your energy and brings you joy is unique to you. Give yourself permission to let go of your business self for a few hours and focus only on your personal life. You will not regret it.

I know many people who think exercise and self-care are important but still don't schedule time for them because they are afraid their business will suffer. Not so! Regular self-care will also improve your business. If you don't believe me, try scheduling time for at least three days a week of exercise for an entire month. At the end of the month, honestly ask yourself if you have been more or less productive, happy, and rested. I know from helping countless coaching clients and from my own experience that you will feel like you have *more* time in your day, not less.

With your new, exceptional staff members working diligently in your business and your renewed focus on practicing self-care and living the life you've always dreamed about, your hiring journey can truly be your very own life-changing hiring success story.

Kristin's Story:

Before I made the big leap from working seven days a week to working three days a week in my pet business, I told myself that, if I wanted to work more days again after trying my new three-day-a-week schedule, I could. Giving myself an "out" to go back to the old schedule was one way I pushed through my fear of stepping away from the business. As it turned out, I didn't want to work more days, and I never went back to working more than three days a week except for a couple of weeks during each year when my managers needed a vacation and only if there was no one but me to fill in.

For the first few months of my new schedule, I just needed to relax and give myself lots of self-care. All that overworking had exhausted me. I needed to give my body, mind, and spirit a lot of time to just be. On my days off, I took walks in the woods, napped, went to movies during the day (such a treat!), and enjoyed lunch with friends.

This three-day schedule would never have happened if I hadn't worked the "delegation muscle" as I mentioned in Chapter 17. Taking the plunge to create a new schedule for myself by letting others do a lot of what I'd been handling myself up until then was not easy! But was it worth it? Absolutely!

Hiring Success Stories:

"Thanks to having wonderful help, I can be mom to my kids first. I can take time off when needed and also have the support system when situations come up. Another benefit is that having them come on board with their own strengths and perspectives has helped our company grow and be more well-rounded."
Julie Graves – Julie's Pet Sitting
Corona, California

"It has been a long process of letting go for me. I now feel comfortable with the two staff members that are doing pet visits. I have some favorite pets that I usually care for, but after 10 years in business, I need time off. I also have a woman who is helping me with scheduling and doing meet and greets when I feel overwhelmed or need time off. I am finally getting my 'life' back."
Kelly McKinney Hall – Kelly's Pet Sitting, LLC
Medford, Oregon

"Hiring staff has allowed us to expand our service area and take on clients we otherwise may not have been able to accommodate. Having additional staff had allowed more free time across the board – not only for myself, but also for each other. Around the holidays, we were able to give each person time with family; some scheduled for lunch and others for dinner. We all have time for vacations and afternoons or days off. We hired an office assistant to help with bookkeeping – something many pet sitters overlook. I make the deposits and she handles entering them in and making sure all invoices have been paid so I am focused on pets, not billing. Running a business alone is all-consuming at some point, and various areas suffer because of it. Hiring staff allows the excellent standard of care we are known for to continue."
Jamie Hoad – Lazy Days Pet Sitting
Rocky Mount, North Carolina

Action Step

In your hiring success journal, make a list of the personal and professional benefits you've experienced since hiring so far. How does the list compare to the goals you recorded in your hiring success journal after reading Chapter 1? Next, make a list of changes you would like to see in your business or personal life as a result of hiring. What actions do you need to take for those changes to become a reality?

Action Step

Self-care will be an important part of your personal and professional growth. Choose one or two nurturing activities from the list suggested in the "Practice Regular Self-Care" section of the chapter and set aside a few hours this week to replenish and restore your mind and body. Commit to at least one self-care action each week and write down what you plan to do (and when) to care for yourself in your hiring success journal.

Action Step

Set your timer for 20 minutes and write in your hiring success journal about the hiring process and what you've learned in your hiring process so far. Reflect on your goals when you first started reading this book and how your business has changed since then. Allow yourself to really think back over the progress and changes you've made. What is going well? What part of your hiring journey still needs work?

NINETEEN

The Final Step

Finishing Your Hiring Journey (for Now)

"Whether you think you can or think you can't, you're right."
–Henry Ford

As you read the final pages of this book, I hope you are feeling a great sense of accomplishment. If you feel a little bit exhausted at this point, don't worry. Hiring exceptional staff members for your business, and trusting them with your clients, takes a certain amount of energy and effort. As you experience the benefits of hiring outlined in Chapter 18, you will probably see all of the time and energy you gave to the process return back to you ... and then some!

Whether you've completely revolutionized your business through hiring or just dipped a toe in the waters of change, take a moment to reflect on what you've learned about your business and about yourself. I've asked you to be really honest with yourself throughout the process. Review your hiring success journal as you reflect on what you've discovered along the way to capture as much knowledge and wisdom as you can from your hiring experience.

Following this chapter, you will find answers to many of the questions I hear from my coaching clients about hiring and a list of resources I recommend. If you find yourself with a question about hiring — either now or as you go through the hiring process again in the future — check the *Questions & Answers* section to see if other pet business owners have asked me the same question. I've included answers to questions that were too specific to warrant their own chapter or section but are important, nonetheless. Both the *Questions & Answers* and *Recommended Resources* sections will give you continued guidance as you continue to grow your hiring muscles.

This is the end of the book, but there is no true end to your hiring journey until the day that you walk away from business ownership completely. I encourage you to continue to use both this book and your hiring success journal as the needs of your business change over time. Remember, this is *your* hiring journey. Enjoy the journey and enjoy the additional time and freedom you are creating with each hire!

Hiring Q&A

These questions and answers come directly from the many hours I have spent coaching clients through their hiring dilemmas and concerns. I hope their questions and my answers will give you further clarity in your own hiring journey.

Job Postings and Finding the Best Staff

Q: How can I make my job posting stand out?

A: The first thing you should look at is the overall "feeling" of your ad. When I was hiring for my own pet business, I wanted my staff to have a great working experience with me, so I stated that in my ad. I also made sure that my ad conveyed a feeling of harmony and great communication. Really look at your values in relation to your staff and how well you treat them, and then let that be a part of your ad. If you are committed to staff communication or well-being, don't be afraid to say so. Your ad will stand out when you let potential applicants know that you are really committed to them enjoying working with you and with your pet and human clients.

Q: I'm not having much success advertising on Craigslist. What do you recommend? Should I put an ad in the local paper?

A: I do not recommend newspaper ads unless you're in a really small town where there is a weekly or daily newspaper and you're certain that the paper gets read. If Craigslist isn't giving you the applicants you are looking for, ask permission to put flyers at veterinarians' and groomers' offices that say "dog walker and pet sitter wanted" and have tear-off tabs with your contact information. If you contact your local rescue group or shelter, you may find they have newsletters that they send out. You could ask them if they would be willing to put an ad in their newsletter for a fee. This will help you target pet lovers!

And don't give up on Craigslist. I work with a lot of people who get frustrated because they may have put ads on Craigslist a couple of times with little response. But then they put a third ad up a few months later and end up finding somebody great. Just like dating, hiring is often a numbers game! Be willing to keep trying Craigslist, even if you are trying other things at the same time, too.

Q: When hiring, am I better off hiring staff with no experience and training them myself or hiring somebody who has a lot of experience?

A: One of the tricky things about hiring somebody that has a lot of experience is that they might be more likely to start their own business down the road. I have often found that the people that I had to train to be pet sitters or dog walkers ended up staying with me longer than those who had extensive pet sitting and dog walking experience. Even though it was more work for me to train them at the beginning, it ended up being more cost effective in the long run (and clients appreciate the consistency when it comes to long-term staff, as well).

As mentioned in the book, paying for your staff to get animal behavior training or to learn pet CPR will greatly benefit your company, and your clients will appreciate your staff members' continuing education. Alternatively, you can hire a skilled dog trainer or cat behaviorist to teach private classes to your staff so they can develop the skills needed to care for pets.

Q: How do I find quality candidates that are willing to accept part-time work and irregular hours?

A: Just be upfront in your job posting and interviews. Clarity will serve both you and the prospective staff member. Include the words "supplemental, part-time income" in your job posting if that's what you're looking for in an applicant. In the ad, I also recommend that you state a specific amount of money or hours that are available in order to be even clearer. You could write something like this in your ad (and/or tell the applicant in person): "You may make anywhere from $20 to $200 per week." That way, they're sure to understand that it's going to be different from week to week. Let them know that you need somebody who can start off slow and add hours as business increases.

Even if you've clearly noted this information in the help wanted ad, you should also verbally state this same information when you're conducting in-person interviews because you don't want to go through the trouble of hiring someone who may have unrealistic expectations or has forgotten how much work is actually available. You want them to understand that you may not have a lot of work for them right now or you may not call them for a while during a slow period. If you are planning to actively market to get more clients after they are hired, go ahead and tell them that, too.

Q: Can I hire somebody who also works for my competitor and wants more part-time hours?

A: You can, but I don't recommend doing so because of the potential conflict of interest. When a staff member is juggling the expectations of two different employers, it's all too likely that they will get double-booked, forget an appointment and/or just not be available to do a job for your client. I've seen this become a big mess for those business owners who have hired people who also work for other companies. It's just not worth the hassle.

Sending Staff to Client Interviews

Q: Should I schedule a second meet-and-greet with my existing clients and a brand new staff member who is going to be caring for their pets?

A: Yes, I would recommend another meet-and-greet once you have a new staff member to take over that current client's walks and visits. It's a nice way for you to make sure the transition is a smooth one for both the client and the staff member.

Q: Do I need to pay my staff members for client meet-and-greets?

A: You absolutely (and legally) need to pay employees for their time, even when they're being trained. Even though it's not legally required that you pay independent contractors for meet-and-greets, I recommend paying them to meet new clients because it shows respect for their time and energy.

Q: What about when it's a current client that I've had for years? Do I still pay staff members for those meet-and-greets?

A: You wouldn't want to charge your client again (if you charge your client for meet-and-greets), but you do need to pay your staff member. Employees must always be paid for their time. With ICs, you can think of it as an investment in staff satisfaction. They will appreciate being paid for their time, and their job satisfaction will pay off for your business in the long run.

Q: How can I make sure my staff members are safe meeting new customers alone? Should I send them in pairs or do all of the meet-and-greets myself? I don't feel comfortable sending a single employee into an unknown situation alone.

A: In the 18 years I had staff working for me, I had pet sitters and dog walkers go to thousands of meet and greets and nothing happened to a staff member in all those years! That's not to say that I didn't have that concern. However, what I always told my staff was that if they ever felt uncomfortable, they never had to take a client they didn't want to take. That was a policy that I upheld. I also let them know they didn't even have to tell me *why* they didn't want a particular client. But one thing I did ask them to do was to let me know immediately upon leaving the client meet-and-greet, if that was the case.

Helping Clients Transition to New Staff

Q: I'm thinking about hiring for the first time, but some of my clients are very particular. I'm not sure they would be comfortable with me hiring someone else because they are used to me. How do I prepare them for the fact that someone other than me will be caring for their home and pets in order to help them feel more comfortable with this change?

A: I recommend that you start by telling them you'd like to have another person trained to care for their home and pets so that when you go on vacation or you're sick, they won't be left without anybody to help in their time of need. Wording it in a positive way will help them see how your hiring helps them, too.

The biggest impact that you can make on your clients who are really challenged by not having you care for their pets anymore is raving about the pet sitter or dog walker you're hiring to replace you. This is why you really want to hire phenomenal people—you're going to be "selling" your clients on them, and it's really important that your confidence in them comes through in your voice and in your interaction with your client. If you don't truly believe the positive description of your new staff member, your clients will probably sense that. You really want to feel good about who you hire so that your clients will too.

Q: What do I say if a client is resistant to a new staff member that doesn't have much experience?

A: First off, always be honest. If you don't, it's going to come back to bite you in the butt. Dishonesty always does! If your new pet sitter or dog walker doesn't have any professional experience but has a lot of experience caring for their own pets, let clients know that. Even while being completely honest, however, focus on building up something that is attractive about your new staff member—her level of love for pets, his ability to provide excellent care, her dependability, etc. Do whatever you can to convey your complete confidence in your staff to your clients.

Paying Staff

Q: If a staff member visits the same client three times a day, should they be paid the same amount as if they had three different clients that day?

A: If the time amounts are the same for each visit then yes, absolutely. A lot of pet sitting and dog walking business owners will offer a discount to the client for multiple visits in the same day or multiple walks each week, but I don't recommend that because it can eat into the bottom line profit margin for both you and your staff. The pet sitters and dog walkers are doing the same amount of work at each visit and need to be paid accordingly. Don't discount their time and energy.

Recommended Resources

I've organized the resources recommended here by the chapter in which I mentioned them. That way, you can refer back to this list easily while you work through the book or when you want to find a resource quickly later on. Because the resources are organized by chapter, you will find some resources listed more than once. That just means they will be helpful to you in more than one part of your hiring journey.

I've included links to the applicable websites for each resource, but if you find that any of the links have changed when you want to access a particular resource, simply do an internet search for the resource name to find the current website.

Introduction: Before You Begin...

Hiring Handbook Facebook Group: Join the private Facebook group specifically for readers of *The Hiring Handbook for Pet Sitters and Dog Walkers* to connect with other pet business owners and share hiring ideas, get questions answered, and celebrate successes. www.facebook.com/groups/PetSitHiringHandbook

Chapter Three: Decide How Much Help You Need

Administration Software: Administration software programs specific to pet sitting and dog walking often include an income-tracking feature that will sort income by service. Email me at Success@SFPSA.com if you want my software recommendation.

QuickBooks: This all-in-one accounting software will track expenses, generate reports, organize receipts, and track taxes. It even has features specifically designed for managing 1099 contractor pay. www.quickbooks.com

Chapter Four: Independent Contractors vs. Employees

Form SS-8, Determination of Worker Status for Purposes of Federal Employment Taxes and Income Tax Withholding: After you submit this form, the IRS will review the specifics of your situation and officially determine whether your worker is an independent contractor or traditional employee. www.irs.gov/forms-pubs/about-form-ss-8

LegalZoom: You can access reduced-cost and prepaid legal help through LegalZoom without going through the traditional process of hiring a lawyer. www.legalzoom.com

SCORE (Service Corps of Retired Executives): This organization offers free legal and other professional support, and you may be able to find a retired employment attorney you can consult with for free. www.score.org

Voluntary Classification Settlement Program: If you determine that your independent contractors have been improperly classified and should be employees instead, the Voluntary Classification Settlement Program gives you the chance to reclassify your workers with partial relief from federal employment taxes and fees. www.irs.gov/forms-pubs/about-form-8952

Chapter Five: Prepare for the Business Side of Hiring

Business Insurance: If you don't currently have an insurance company you are satisfied with, or are planning to shop around to compare rates through a pet sitting association, send me an email at Success@SFPSA.com for my business insurance recommendation.

Employer Identification Number: If you haven't already, apply for an EIN with the IRS. Set up a record-keeping system for each employee's file. Download any tax forms you need at www.irs.gov/forms.

FreshBooks: FreshBooks is an online accounting program that will let you track times and create professional invoices directly from your phone. www.freshbooks.com

Healthcare.gov: Resources and discounts for small businesses that want or need to provide health insurance to employees can be found here. www.healthcare.gov/small-businesses

LegalZoom: You can access reduced-cost and prepaid legal help through LegalZoom without going through the traditional process of hiring a lawyer. www.legalzoom.com

QuickBooks: This all-in-one accounting software will track expenses, generate reports, organize receipts, and track taxes. It even has features specifically designed for managing 1099 contractor pay. www.quickbooks.com

SCORE (Service Corps of Retired Executives): This organization offers free legal and other professional support, and you may be able to find a retired employment attorney you can consult with for free. www.score.org

Chapter Six: Pay Your Staff

Minimum Wage: You can view minimum wage laws by state on the U.S. Department of Labor's website. www.dol.gov/whd/minwage

Rate Increase Letter: If you haven't increased your prices in a while, or if you need suggestions on the best ways to notify your clients of the price increase, you will find a sample rate increase email template at the bottom of the "Free Stuff" page of my website: www.SFPSA.com/free.

Wage Webinars: To help my coaching clients navigate the legal side of staffing and pay, I have a number of hiring webinar recordings for pet sitters and dog walkers available for purchase on my website. Some of these recordings talk specifically about wage laws. You'll find the recordings near the bottom of this page: www.SFPSA.com/hire.

Chapter Seven: Harness the Power of an Application Packet

Application Packet: My fully customizable Application Packet for Hiring Pet Sitters and Dog Walkers is available on my website if you would prefer to purchase one instead of creating your own. www.SFPSA.com/packet

Chapter Eight: Find Exceptional Pet Sitters and Dog Walkers

Sample Job Postings: An electronic template of the two ads in this chapter, as well as an overnight pet sitter advertisement, are available for purchase as part of the comprehensive hiring kit, or each ad can be purchased individually. www.SFPSA.com/hire

Chapter Nine: Interview with Confidence

Insight Timer: Intentional mindfulness through meditation will help you learn to recognize and trust your intuition. Insight Timer is an app that walks you through guided meditation as you build that intuition muscle. www.insighttimer.com

Chapter Ten: Get New Staff Members Started Off Right

Employee Handbook: A ready-made employee handbook that is fully customizable for your business is available to purchase. www.SFPSA.com/welcome

LegalZoom: You can access reduced-cost and prepaid legal help through LegalZoom without going through the traditional process of hiring a lawyer. www.legalzoom.com

SCORE (Service Corps of Retired Executives): This organization offers free legal and other professional support, and you may be able to find a retired employment attorney you can consult with for free. www.score.org

Welcome Packet for the New Staff Member: A customizable version of my Welcome Packet for the New Staff Member is for sale at the website www.SFPSA.com/welcome.

Alternatively, the Welcome Packet is also included as part of the complete Hiring Kit for Pet Sitting and Dog Walking Staff here: www.SFPSA.com/hire.

Chapter Eleven: Schedule Staff for Success

Administration Software: A scheduling and administration software program specific to pet sitting and dog walking can be very helpful to you as you schedule staff members. Email me at Success@SFPSA.com if you want my most current recommendation.

Bitrix24: This is an all-in-one communication program for businesses that includes a calendar, group chat (and video), and a Customer Relationship Management (CRM) system built right in. www.bitrix24.com

Google Calendar: Coordinate your personal and professional calendars and send reminders to everyone who subscribes to the calendar for free with Google Calendar. www.google.com/calendar

Google Docs: Easy document storage and great for sharing information with a group. www.google.com/docs

WhatsApp Business: Communicate with customers and staff members easily with this internet-based calling and messaging program. One especially helpful feature is the option to tag contacts and messages with specific labels for easy organization. www.whatsapp.com/business

Chapter Fourteen: How to Let Staff Go

LegalZoom: You can access reduced-cost and prepaid legal help through LegalZoom without going through the traditional process of hiring a lawyer. www.legalzoom.com

New Staff Member Contract: Containing both an employee and IC contract, the New Staff Member Contract was designed specifically for pet sitters and dog walkers and is fully customizable for your business. www.SFPSA.com/employee

SCORE (Service Corps of Retired Executives): This organization offers free legal and other professional support, and you may be able to find a retired employment attorney you can consult with for free. www.score.org

Chapter Fifteen: Protect Your Business Reputation

Administration Software: Some scheduling and administration software programs specific to pet sitting and dog walking include staff monitoring services. Email me at Success@SFPSA.com for my software recommendation.

Hellotracks: Designed for field-based industries (as opposed to office-based businesses), this location service will let you track and communicate with staff members easily when they are on the job. www.hellotracks.com

HubStaff: HubStaff is a complete employee coordination system with everything from GPS tracking to online time sheets. It also integrates directly with QuickBooks, which is a huge time saver if you already use that accounting software. www.hubstaff.com

MailChimp: MailChimp is a web-based service specifically designed to facilitate marketing through email newsletters, surveys, and more. www.mailchimp.com

SurveyMonkey: This site enables you to create your own client questionnaires from scratch or using one of countless available templates. SurveyMonkey is also optimized for mobile surveys if you want to expand into quick surveys that clients can take directly from their phones. www.surveymonkey.com

Welcome Packet for the New Staff Member: A customizable version of my Welcome Packet for the New Staff Member is for sale at the website www.SFPSA.com/welcome.

Alternatively, the Welcome Packet is also included as part of the complete Hiring Kit for Pet Sitting and Dog Walking Staff here: www.SFPSA.com/hire.

Chapter Sixteen: Hire Help for the Business Side of Running a Business

Hours: This time-tracking app makes it easy for you to keep track of what you do (and how long it takes) on any given workday. This is especially helpful for figuring out what to ask your office managers to do for you ... and about how long it will take once they learn how to do it. You can even add notes to specific activities, making it even simpler to train your staff on a particular job. www.hourstimetracking.com

LegalZoom: You can access reduced-cost and prepaid legal help through LegalZoom without going through the traditional process of hiring a lawyer. www.legalzoom.com

Office Manager/Administrative Assistant Manual: My comprehensive guide and customizable manual for the office duties of your office manager or administrative assistant, based on the manual I gave my own office managers. www.SFPSA.com/manager

Office Manager Hiring Kit: A comprehensive hiring kit for office managers and administrative assistants which includes a customizable job posting, application packet, and manager manual that you can customize for your business needs. www.SFPSA.com/manager

SCORE (Service Corps of Retired Executives): This organization offers free legal and other professional support, and you may be able to find a retired employment attorney you can consult with for free. www.score.org

Tools for Start-Up, Growth Acceleration, and Hiring

Thousands of pet sitters and dog walkers from all over the world have used the Six-Figure Pet Sitting Academy™ Pet Sitting and Dog Walking Start-Up Kit, Business Hiring Kit, client contracts, hiring tools, and success recordings to start and grow their pet businesses. And you can too!

The site contains over forty pet sitting and dog walking business forms and tools that can help you get started or expand your business — right now!

All products are available for instant download so you'll receive the items you order in less than sixty seconds. Also, all start-up and hiring kits, client contracts, and forms are fully editable so you can customize as needed for your business.

Find out more about the products that can take your pet business to the next level:

www.SFPSA.com/petsit

4-Week Pet Business Online Group Programs

Do you need support to create a profitable and easy-to-run business *and* a great life?

I offer online pet business programs, and you are welcome to join me and other pet sitting and dog walking business owners from around the world who are excited to create a successful business and fulfilling life. Each program has a private Facebook group to keep you connected and feeling supported long after the programs are over.

These are virtual programs, and they are designed so you can participate from anywhere in the world. You can even attend from your pet sitting or dog walking office or from your car! And if you miss a class, no problem — the recording will be available for you to watch, listen, and learn from whenever you like.

The **Catapult 4-Week Pet Business Bootcamp** is for pet sitters and dog walkers who want to launch their business into greater success with ease.

The **Jumpstart 4-Week Pet Business Burnout Recovery Program** is a recovery course for pet business owners suffering from pet business burnout (you know who you are).

The **30 Days to Start and Grow Your Pet Sitting and Dog Walking Business Program** is designed for anyone who wants

to take the dream of owning a pet sitting and dog walking business from idea to reality in 30 days, within the supportive and accountable framework of a weekly course, surrounded by like-minded pet business entrepreneurs who really "get it".

You can learn more about the online programs, read testimonials from past graduates, and sign up now by visiting the pages below:

Catapult 4-Week Pet Business Bootcamp:

www.SFPSA.com/catapult

Jumpstart 4-Week Pet Business Burnout Recovery Program:

www.SFPSA.com/jump

30 Days to Start and Grow Your Pet Sitting and Dog Walking Business Online Program:

www.SFPSA.com/30

Prosperous Pet Business Podcast

Each month, I release podcast episodes to help you in your pet sitting and dog walking business journey (and in your personal life). There are a lot of podcast episodes already available and waiting for you, and they are all free. Check them out!

You can listen by subscribing on your favorite podcast service or by visiting the Prosperous Pet Business podcast page:

www.prosperouspetbusiness.com/pet-business-podcast

Enjoy, and happy listening and learning!

Prosperous Pet Business Online Conference

Every year, I interview pet business experts and offer those valuable interviews for FREE at an annual online conference that is just for pet business owners. Find out more and sign up here:

www.prosperouspetbusiness.com

FREE Six-Figure Pet Sitting Academy Resources

Find a free sample rate increase letter on the SFPSA Resources page:

www.SFPSA.com/resources

Visit the Six-Figure Pet Sitting Academy blog for business tips, tools and articles on how to create a pet sitting business beyond your wildest dreams!

www.SFPSA.com/blog

Sign up for the FREE Six-Figure Business Tips and Tools Newsletter:

www.SFPSA.com

I would love to hear how this book has helped you hire exceptional new employees and find more peace and freedom in your business!

Email me your success story: success@SFPSA.com

Connect with me and Six-Figure Pet Sitting Academy on these social media sites:

Follow me on Facebook:
www.Facebook.com/SixFigurePetSittingAcademy

Join my private Facebook group for readers of this book:
www.Facebook.com/groups/PetSitHiringHandbook

Instagram: www.Instagram.com/PetBizCoach

LinkedIn: www.LinkedIn.com/in/SixFigurePetSitting

Pinterest: www.Pinterest.com/SixFigurePetBiz

Twitter: @PetSittingCoach

About the Author

Kristin Morrison started her pet sitting and dog walking company in 1995 and it grew to be one of the largest pet care companies in California. She hired over 250 pet sitters and dog walkers during the course of running her business. When she sold her business in 2013, it had grown to include 35 staff members and 4 managers.

Since 2000, Kristin has provided pet business coaching for thousands of pet sitters, dog walkers, and other service-based pet business owners across the United States, Canada, the UK, and Australia. In 2008, she founded Six-Figure Pet Sitting Academy™, which provides coaching, webinars, and business products for pet sitters and dog walkers. She also created Six-Figure Pet Business Academy™ for all service-based pet business owners, including dog trainers, pet groomers, and dog daycare owners.

Kristin is a nationally recognized speaker at pet business conferences and for pet business networking groups. She also hosts the annual Prosperous Pet Business Online Conference and the Prosperous Pet Business podcast. Kristin has written four additional books for pet business owners: *30 Days to Start and Grow Your Pet Sitting and Dog Walking Business*, *Six-Figure Pet Sitting*, the *Prosperous Pet Business: Interviews with the Experts* series, and *Six-Figure Pet Business*. Kristin lives in Marin County, California, with her husband, Spencer.

CPSIA information can be obtained
at www.ICGtesting.com
Printed in the USA
LVHW020431281022
731594LV00009B/717